Inviting God In

Inviting God In

Scriptural Reflections and Prayers
Throughout the Year

Joyce Rupp

ave maria press
Notre Dame, Indiana

Many of these devotions and prayers were first printed in *Living Faith: Daily Catholic Devotions* published quarterly by Creative Communications for the Parish, Inc., 1564 Fencorp Drive, Fenton, MO 63026, 1-800-325-9414.

First Printing, July 2001
Third Printing, April 2002
45,000 copies in print

www.avemariapress.com

International Standard Book Number: 0-87793-958-6

Cover design by Brian Conley
Text design by Mark Neilsen
Interior illustrations by Sally Beck

Printed and bound in the United States of America.

Library of Congress Cataloging-in-Publication Data
Rupp, Joyce.
    Inviting God in : scriptural reflections and prayers throughout the year / Joyce Rupp.
    p. cm.
    Includes index.
    ISBN 0-87793-958-6 (pbk.)
    1. Church year meditations. 2. Bible--Meditations. 3. Catholic Church--Prayer-books and devotions--English.   I. Title.
    BX2170.C55 R86 2001
    242'.3--dc21
                                                                              2001002636
                                                                                   CIP

*Dedicated to each person
who has used* Living Faith
*as a daily guide and source
of spiritual nurturance.*

Contents

Preface

Ten years ago when I opened the letter from Creative Communications for the Parish inviting me to write meditations for *Living Faith,* I hesitated. I wasn't sure I wanted the commitment, and I knew most certainly that I did not want any more writing deadlines. But as I pondered the possibility of reflecting on the scriptures, I decided it would be good for my spiritual growth to do so. I had been inspired and nurtured often by pondering scriptural texts. It seemed there was always another insight, another morsel of nurturance in a scripture passage, no matter how often I visited the same one. So I said "yes" to the offer in hopes that my reflections would be helpful for myself and for others as well.

Thus began the unfolding of the meditations contained in this book. Every three months I was assigned to reflect on specific scripture readings for five days of the liturgical season. I never knew what passages I would be given until I opened the envelope. Soon after the letter arrived, I would sit down with my Bible and begin to read and reflect on these passages. Each time I did so, it felt to me as though I was opening the door of my life and inviting God to come in and be present with me. I knew for certain the insights and spiritual nudges I received were not due to my efforts alone.

What you find in this book is the result of those many times of inviting God to be with me as I pondered the scriptures. The meditations have all been published in *Living Faith,* a booklet that contains brief meditations on the daily scripture readings in the Lectionary. You will note that certain feast days or liturgical seasons may not contain as many reflections as you would anticipate or hope to have. This is because I have prayed and written about the passages that were assigned to me rather than ones I might have chosen myself.

What I did not know ten years ago is how many people use *Living Faith* for their daily prayer. I cannot begin to tell you how much it means to me to know that over 600,000 booklets are printed for each issue. The thought that throughout the world there are people who desire to grow spiritually and are hungry enough for God that they would take time to reflect on a scripture passage each day is simply astounding and immensely hopeful to me. What a great spiritual bond we have.

In the numerous retreats and conferences that I give in the U.S. and Canada as well as Europe, Australia and New Zealand, participants tell me that they read the daily meditations and are helped by them. I also receive countless letters from *Living Faith* readers. It is humbling to receive these messages in which many tell me their life situations of struggle and pain, insight and renewal. One of the most rewarding letters I received was from a man who was in prison. While I rarely maintain an extended correspondence with those who write to me, I have done so with this person. He is now out of prison and the spiritual growth that was encouraged by his use of *Living Faith* has continued to develop and deepen for him.

As I look back on the past ten years of my association with *Living Faith*, I have a clearer picture of the value of this small booklet. I see that whenever we take time to pray with the scripture of the day it is like coming to the table of the Holy One. When we deliberately pause to nourish our spirit, we are saying by our action that we desire spiritual growth. I know God is already present with us but we are not always present to God. So when we turn our minds and hearts to intentionally connect with the divine Presence, we are welcoming the One who is waiting to enrich us and gift us with growth.

The process of creating these meditations has been a blessing for me. As with all good and growthful experiences I have often had the help and influence of others. I am especially grateful to Mark Neilsen, my editor, who suggested that we gather the meditations I had written for *Living Faith* and print them as a collection. Through the years I have worked closely with Mark and I value his integrity and his editorial abilities. It has been a great joy to know and work with him on this book as well as on the daily reflections for *Living Faith*.

As I edited the meditations and added or expanded the accompanying prayers, I thought of how this book could be of benefit. Hopefully it will be read and prayed by individuals who are seeking to nurture their daily life. It could also serve as a catalyst for those preparing worship services and other prayer experiences. May what is contained here be a source of inspiration and a support for all who invite God into their lives.

Joyce Rupp, osm

Prayer: God's Gift to Us

The beginning of prayer

In *Letters to a Young Poet*, the poet Rainer Maria Rilke urges the young writer to want to write so much that he cannot *not* write. That's what happened to me. I eventually longed so much to write that I simply had to write.

The same is true for prayer. We need to come to a point in our lives when we want to pray so much that we cannot imagine a day in which we do not have a time and a place for God.

How does this kind of commitment happen? It is obviously a gift from God. We can't force this sort of desire on ourselves. It happens in its own good time. It is God's power working through us, which "can do more than we can ever ask or imagine" (Ephesians 3:20).

How to pray better

We can't do prayer alone. We can't coerce and shove our way into a relationship with God. Learning to pray takes a lifetime of openness and hope and it is especially challenging when the last thing we want to do is pray. One of the best ways to make ourselves available to a deepening friendship, however, is spending time with the other person. Each day prayer requires a genuine openness of mind and heart and a heartfelt intention to be more at home with God.

Who we understand God to be makes a tremendous difference in why and how we pray. There are as many ways to approach or name God as there are people in the universe. The Scriptures are filled with descriptions of this mysterious Presence in our midst. I have personally come to believe that the most powerful descriptions of God are: "I am who I am" (Exodus 3:14) and "I have loved you" (John 15:12). God is mystery. God is love. It is enough, more than enough, for me to know these two beautiful facets of Divine Goodness.

Approaching such a mysterious God

I used to be afraid of God, fearful of what demands and difficult tests God might ask of me if I got too close. I didn't trust God with my life. When I came to know God as One who is always for me and never against me (Romans 8:31-39), then I was able to walk in peace. God is *with* me, *for* me, dwelling *within* me. God is not "out there" somewhere. What a difference this makes in a relationship if God is understood to be near and not far away. When I pray, I like to image myself being filled with and surrounded by this great Love.

A speaker once described our relationship with God as that of a sponge in an ocean of love. We are each a sponge filled with the Ocean of Love but the Ocean is so much more than each of us.

Finding the time to pray

We live in a world filled with activity. There's nothing wrong with that. Activity and everyday endeavors can be healthy dimensions of life because this is where we are and where God is. It is out of this very nitty-gritty and whirlwind life that our spiritual growth can happen. Hurry and busyness, however, get to be unhealthy when we allow our activities to steal all our time away so that we never look inside to that wonderful world of the soul. Busyness may appear to be very legitimate when, in reality, it is our excuse for not praying because we don't feel like praying, don't know how to pray or wonder if anything happens when we pray.

We need to want to pray enough to set aside a time and place each day to be alone with God, our Beloved Companion. As in a marriage, if we just breeze by our Companion every day with only a nod or a kiss of hello and good-bye, the relationship can easily slip into artificiality and lack depth because we have not shared anything of our inner self.

Spiritual writer José Hobday once said that every person ought to spend as much time in prayer as in eating. Now that's a challenge! Yet, it rings true: We take the time to feed the hungers of our body, but so often neglect the hungers of our soul.

Trying to pray on a regular basis

What often keeps a person from daily prayer is the belief that one has to follow through perfectly or exactly every day. For instance, someone might decide to pray for fifteen minutes every morning. After two days of this, one of the children is ill, and there goes the fifteen minutes. The next morning it may be a flat tire or some other household emergency that takes another fifteen minutes.

Rather than say, "It's no use, I can't find time to pray," this person needs to say, "Well, I wasn't able to have the space the last two days, but I can today . . . and I will. I'll begin again today."

Spiritual growth doesn't just happen. It means not answering the phone or door during one's special time of prayer, not giving in to the long list of "must do's" which come to mind when we are finally quiet, and asking family members to respect one's quiet time by not interfering unless it's a *real* emergency.

When it is difficult to concentrate on prayer

Distractions and boredom are often seen as key "enemies" of prayer. I think, instead, that each of these enemies can be a helpful teacher. What if I am at prayer and I keep trying to be still and listen to God and all that happens is that I keep feeling angry at someone? Maybe this is God's way of telling me that I need to send loving thoughts toward that person, or let go of my anger and offer forgiveness, or find the courage to make a decision to go to that person to work out our differences.

Sometimes distractions are a gift from our memory. It may be something like "Oh, I forgot to take the bread out of the freezer!" When this happens, all we need do is write down a brief reminder on a pad of paper and go on with our quiet time.

Our minds will usually be quite active when we go to our time of prayer. It can help to use "centering prayer" which consists of saying a word or phrase to name God as we breathe in and breathe out. I personally find it very helpful to focus simply on my breath when my mind is filled with chatter. Sometimes I use Thich Nhat Hanh's suggestion of saying "yes" to the gift of life as I breathe in, and "thank you" for all that has been given as I breathe out.

When prayer gets tedious

Boredom may be telling us that we need to enliven our prayer, try some new approaches, be open to a different way to envision God, or be more open and honest with God. Boredom may be telling us that our human spirit is at a low point physically, mentally or emotionally. It may be teaching us patient endurance or faithfulness.

Boredom may be trying to draw us into accepting the "being" aspect of prayer which is very difficult for Americans who always want something to show for their efforts.

Boredom and not wanting to pray might be teaching us that we have to let go of thinking that we are the ones who make prayer happen. It could be a very graced time of learning how to surrender to God, the source of our growth.

When I think of "prayer," I think of the many ways a relationship develops. Certainly it happens through speaking to another person. It is also essential that it involve *listening*. How much more difficult to listen than to speak. More difficult yet is being at ease in a relationship when two persons are silent together.

Prayer is being with God in an *intentional* way. In other words, I can deliberately turn my mind and heart toward God in whatever I am involved. I can relate to God anytime and anywhere. As I prepare a meal, I can deliberately recall how God is with me. Prayer can take place as I enjoy the muscles and mobility of the human body or the beauty of winter snow. It might happen as I drive to work and sense God's love encompassing all who are on the freeway. Or when I am in the shower and I offer to God all that I am and all that I have as I begin the day.

Sometimes we are "pulled" into prayer, so to speak, when a sunset or a mountain or a newborn child catches our spirit and tumbles us into a deep awareness of Someone besides ourselves being there.

How to relate to God in prayer

We know intellectually that prayer is more than just talking to God or simply asking for things. No healthy relationship consists of only these things. But relating to God in other ways is difficult because this little voice in us doubts the value of prayer when all one is doing is being present to God's presence.

We know in our heads, but perhaps not in our hearts, that prayer is not about good feelings. Our relationship to God can be vital and dynamic when we are restless, bored, depressed, or empty. Significant spiritual growth can take place in the darkness. We will have times of not feeling good when we are at prayer, but God certainly does not abandon us during these moments. God continues to embrace us as lovingly in the darkness as in the light.

I used to worry and be anxious about my prayer, wondering if it was "good" prayer or not. I'd feel guilty if I came to the close of my prayer time and my mind had been one giant distraction. If I didn't have good feelings, I'd think that maybe I didn't pray well enough or have sufficient desire in my heart. If I was bored or restless or didn't want to be at prayer, I'd chide myself for losing faith or not caring.

Gradually, all that worry and anxiety left me as I recognized that God knows my heart, my desires, my humanness. I won't always have good feelings because I am not always feeling good physically, mentally or emotionally. Life doesn't always have a rosy glow to it. I will not always want to pray because real relationships do not consist of only happy and upbeat times.

What is really essential for prayer?

What is vital to my prayer is that I continue to be faithful to being with God. God wants and needs no more than this from any of us—just our faithful presence. My body can be at prayer and my mind and spirit may keep slipping and sliding with ten thousand distractions, and it is still all right. I keep returning to my intention: to be in union with God, to be present, to be here and now with the One who holds me close and will never let me go, no matter how empty, lonely, distracted, or angry I may feel.

Prayer isn't about God whisking away all the human conditions we are in. Rather, prayer is about this Loving Presence staying with us and never going away. It is about God encouraging and loving us as we attempt to live our lives well. It is about God guiding us and showing us the way in which we are to grow.

This truth helped me to let go of guilt about falling asleep as I prayed my evening prayer. I had the insight one day that it was actually a rather beautiful event, this falling asleep as I prayed. It was like I fell asleep in the arms of God. This thought changed my guilt into gratitude for a kind and welcoming God who understands my weariness.

What, then, is prayer? I think it is summed up in the words from the musical *Godspell*, which are based on a sixteenth-century prayer by Richard Chichester: "Three things I pray: to see Thee more clearly, to love Thee more dearly, to follow Thee more nearly, day by day."

Joyce Rupp, osm

Advent and Christmas

Waiting in Tough Times

■ **Wait for the Lord; be strong, and let your heart take courage; wait for the Lord!** Psalm 27:14

Certain words are employed so often during our liturgical seasons that they can easily be ignored due to overuse. "Waiting" is one of these words. It may also be difficult for us to sense how the people of old waited for a savior. It's quite another thing, though, if we are in the midst of a struggle or a situation where *we* are currently waiting for something painful to change.

I know many people who are waiting. Some have cancer, and are waiting to die. There's a family waiting to be healed of the pain they all experienced when one of their little girls was abused by an uncle. Another person is anxiously waiting to hear if he has the job for which he was recently interviewed. Yet another waits to know if she will have to move away from her home in which she has lived for 30 years.

What does this waiting have to do with longing for God's coming? When we wait in tough times, we are in a special God-moment. We know we can't "go it alone." The One who came into this world is our Peace-bringer. As we wait, we turn to our God and cry out for Peace to come and enfold us.

Source of Peace,
bring your serenity and inner repose
to those who wait to be relieved
of their pain and struggle.

Too Busy to Be Aware of God?

■ **Do not fear, O Zion; do not let your hands grow weak. The Lord, your God, is in your midst.** Zephaniah 3:16-17

Could there be any better time than Advent to focus on and remember that God dwells in our midst? I find it particularly necessary to be aware of God's nearness when I am zooming through December, busy about too many things. It is easy to get swallowed up by my anxiety or discouragement, knowing that I am unable to do all the planning and preparations I would like to do before Christmas comes.

I draw inspiration and encouragement when I recognize that the one whose birth I am preparing to celebrate, dwells in the midst of all my activities and relationships. I have only to open my inner eyes and recognize the presence of God in the love, joy, care, concern, honesty and peace of those around me. I also need to be mindful of how God is present in those who have very little joy because of their physical or mental condition, financial deprivation or the violence of their political situation. It is here that I meet the suffering Christ. Busyness dulls my awareness of the presence of Emmanuel. Excessive attention to material things lessens my bond with God. God is with me, if only I slow down long enough to look and see.

Emmanuel, God-with-us,
let me not be discouraged.
You are in my life.
I will slow down so I can find you there.

What Healing Do I Need?

■ **Great crowds came to him, bringing with them the lame, the maimed, the blind, the mute, and many others. They put them at his feet, and he cured them.** Matthew 15:30

*T*he people brought their wounded to Jesus and laid them at his feet, trusting that his presence and his touch would bring them a better quality of life. These people were given new sight, limbs that worked again, a voice where all had been silent, and good health instead of disease.

Advent is a season of hopeful growth, a time when we can bring to God what is wounded in us and ask for restoration. It is a good time to pause and ask: What is there within my life that I need to bring to the feet of Jesus for healing? Has any part of my life gone lame? Has my enthusiasm waned? My trust in others broken? My energy to do good depleted? Have I been blind to things that need tending in my spirit? Is there a relationship out of place that needs to be restored? Have I lost a voice in what ought to be spoken to another?

I come to you today, Divine Healer,
and lay my life at your feet.
May I be healed of what keeps me
from being more fully yours.
Help me to be spiritually healthy.

Listen Carefully to Find the Way

■ **Your Teacher will not hide . . . but your eyes shall see your Teacher . . . your ears shall hear a word behind you, saying, "This is the way; walk in it."** Isaiah 30:20-21

A group I was with at a retreat had an engaging conversation about how we might "know God's will." We spoke about how difficult it is sometimes to make a decision that might be in keeping with what God would want for us. It's especially hard when all the options seem to be basically good ones. How do we choose? How do we know what God desires for us?

The prophet Isaiah speaks of God as our Teacher. We need to trust that God will be with us in our searching and our decision-making. If we long to follow God's ways, Holy Wisdom will surely guide us and teach us what is best for us.

Isaiah also implies that we need to listen. Rarely will we hear the words of God as clearly as those in Isaiah 30, but if we daily attune to God through prayer, try to be open, be aware of our resistances, and live life as best we can, then I believe we can trust that we will make good decisions.

God my Teacher,
during Advent I ask you to guide me
in your ways and with your wisdom.
I will listen closely deep within myself and trust
you with my life.

Remembering Our Gifted Ancestors

■ **So all the generations from Abraham to David are fourteen generations** . . . Matthew 1:17

When the long line of generations was read during liturgy I used to stifle a yawn. Then one day I realized that the recitation of the ancestral lineage of Jesus could be a powerful spiritual experience of remembering his heritage of faith as well as my own.

I have come to appreciate the power of ancestors from several sources. One of these is from the Native American tradition. They value their spiritual lineage so much that they often begin their rituals by "calling in the ancestors." They believe that there is much inspiration to be gained from remembering the gifted presence of those who had deep faith. I have also felt this power and blessing of presence when my religious community has begun a prayer service by naming our deceased members who left behind such gifted legacies for us. Their strength and goodness inspire and encourage me.

Today, as we listen to or read the ancestral legacy of Jesus, we can pause to be grateful for all those seeds of life and faith that led to the life of Jesus and to our own faith life. Then, we can look and see how we, too, are a part of a lineage of faith that influences those who will come after us.

Source and Root of my faith,
thank you for the ancestors
whose faith has shaped my own
and brought me into union with you.

The Key to Peace of Mind

■ **I will say, "Peace be within you!"** Psalm 122:8

What better time to ponder "peace" than during the busy weeks of Advent as we busily shop, make plans for Christmas gatherings, attend parties, and try to write annual letters to long-forgotten relatives and friends. Ironically, it sometimes feels that peace is far away from our hearts during this frenzied time.

Peace is more than the absence of conflict. It is an attitude about life. The prophet Isaiah writes that those who trust God are the ones who have peace (Isaiah 26:3). We can't keep all the hustle and bustle out of our lives. We can't avoid some daily conflicts and difficulties but we can give ourselves in trust to God. How? Each time we feel distress, act unlovingly, succumb to anxious worrying or get caught in a whirlwind of activity, we can refocus our inner self. We can turn our hearts toward peace by asking ourselves some questions: What will all this mean after I die? What is the value here? What do I need to let go of and entrust to God? Peace of mind and heart is simple. Isaiah knew that. It means trusting that God is with us and that this gift is all we really need for our happiness.

> *God of Peace, do not let me forget*
> *that you are the most essential part of my life.*
> *Keep reorienting me to your presence*
> *as I move through this busy time of year.*

God's Ways of Being Known

■ **There appeared to him an angel of the Lord . . .** Luke 1:11

Angels appear at very significant moments in people's lives. They act as messengers of God, guiding, inviting, protecting, giving directions. Angels offer both comfort and challenge as they bring their messages from God. Currently, angels are "in"—they are everywhere, in films, television, books, art and cards. These angels are often presented as beautiful pieces of art, or as cute cherubs, with no particular reference to anything other than being a source of entertainment or of enjoyment for the eyes. It is easy, amid all this, to forget what angels signify in Scripture. Angels remind us that there is a spiritual realm in our lives where God is always desiring to be known and heard.

This Advent is a good time to be more aware of this spiritual dimension, to be open to hearing the voice of God, to receiving comfort and guidance, whether this comes in prayer or in the hidden disguise of another person who is an unexpected messenger of God for us. Advent is the season to allow ourselves to be drawn toward God by the inner communications that are given to us. Let us be aware and open to the many ways that God desires to enter into our lives.

Thank you, Holy One,
for the surprising ways
you choose to visit my life.
May I be open to your messengers.

Keeping My Heart Open to God

■ . . . **the Lord whom you seek will suddenly come to his temple.** Malachi 3:1

Why do I think that just because I pray faithfully and follow certain prescribed spiritual practices during Advent (or any other time) that God will immediately be revealed to me? Why do I get discouraged when I do not feel joy and enthusiasm as Christmas nears? I get caught off guard by my desire to control my spiritual process. Usually I know very well that I can only be receptive, that I cannot force God, but sometimes I forget and go into a spiritual pout wondering if my prayer life is any good at all.

God will be revealed in the temple of my life when it is God's time for revelation, not when I demand it. My culture tells me that when I work hard, I'll have something to show for it, but this is not God's way. Divine revelation is always a gift, a surprise, a totally unearned happening. My seeking God through prayer and good deeds is simply a way of preparing my heart to be open for the great event of revelation, not a way to get God to give me what I want.

Word Made Flesh,
I wait with hope for your coming
as I turn my heart toward your love.
I seek you and await your revelation
with openness and with confidence.

Always Room for Hope

■ **The Lord God will wipe away the tears from all faces.**
Isaiah 25:8

*T*his particular passage from Isaiah offers a vital component of hope in the season of Advent. It expresses the belief that no matter what happens to us, God will be there to comfort and support us. To maintain hope in our world is sometimes difficult when numerous countries are currently at war and throngs of refugees search for new homes. Finding hope is also difficult in our own sphere of life when we are grieving, struggling with illness, or experiencing some other difficulty that continually erodes our hope.

My friend, hospice nurse Joyce Hutchison, writes that no matter how bad things get for her dying patients, there is always room for hope. Hope changes as their health situation changes, but even a glimmer of hope, such as hoping the sun will shine, helps them find some joy in each day.

Isn't this true for all of us? We hope that nothing bad will ever happen to us; then we hope that we will get through the tough things that do happen; then we hope that God will be there to wipe away our tears as we search for relief and consolation.

God of Hope, lift my drooping spirit
when I am low and losing confidence.
Revive my joy when it fades away.
Call me home to your abiding peace
when I am lost in the realm of chaos.

God Our Rock

■ **Trust in the Lord forever, for in the Lord God you have an everlasting rock.** Isaiah 26:4

*H*ave you ever explored the facets of a rock? If you have, you'll know why God is quite frequently described as "our rock." Rocks are the sturdiest of all created things, existing from earliest times. To destroy a rock is very difficult; wind and water can erode a rock, but it is a very slow process. Strong and enduring, rocks can be used to build walls of great strength and protection. Caves, hollowed out of rock by nature, are great sources of refuge for numerous creatures. These rock formations have also been sheltering homes for many ancient people.

In using a metaphor such as "rock" when we refer to God, we are indicating that we have someone who is a strong support, a sturdy shelter, and a comforting protection for us. It also suggests that we believe in a God who is an eternal refuge, a constant source of strength, one whose love is as enduring as the ancient rocks of the universe.

The next time you see a rock or a large stone, touch it or sit upon it or hold it in your hand. Let it speak to you of the marvels of God our Rock.

God, my rock,
you are my shelter and protection
from the storms of life.
Thank you for being my strength
and a source of resilience.

Stars Reveal a Radiant Presence

■ He determines the number of the stars; he gives to all of them their names. Psalm 147:4

*I*n the time of the psalmist, our scientific knowledge about the many galaxies and vast solar systems of the universe was unavailable. Yet stars have always drawn their viewers to another realm. Stars are used in many places in Scripture to proclaim the wonder and power of God. The vastness of the sky and its stars called to those who were drawn to the divine.

I can easily understand why this is so. I don't think I've ever stood silently beneath a star-filled sky and not felt drawn to a holy Presence. There is an immediate sense of how small I am and how large the universe is. But there is more: I sense a closeness in spite of my smallness. I sense an attraction and a yearning for mystery that far outreaches my rational mind. My whole being is filled with an "ah," and I find myself wanting to kneel before the beauty and mystery of the Creator.

This Advent, go outside on a clear-sky evening (if it's cold, bundle up so you won't be in a hurry to go back inside). Be as still as you can. Look up at the amazing lights of the sky. Welcome again into your heart the Holy One whose radiant presence fills our vast universe.

Creator of the Universe,
my heart resounds with wonder and joy
at the amazing lights placed in the universe.
Their beauty and their brilliance
reflect your divine beauty and glory.

Resting in God's Arms

■ **Comfort, O comfort my people . . . Speak tenderly to Jerusalem.** Isaiah 40:1-2

*T*here are difficult moments in our lives when we need comfort. There are tough times when we yearn for consolation. The suffering people who looked for the long-awaited Messiah were given a hope-filled image of God in the writings of Isaiah. This prophet describes a consoling God who is a shepherd, lovingly looking for and gathering up wandering and homeless sheep in tender arms.

When we are in distress and waiting for consolation, how do we see God with us? Isaiah assures us that God longs to gather us and carry us, to offer guidance and a compassionate heart. What a comforting way to picture God being with us.

Today, imagine yourself experiencing the tenderness of God in one of these ways: resting in God's arms as a weary one would do with a good friend; gathered lovingly by God as a lost sheep would be by a concerned shepherd; consoled by God in an embrace of deep love by the beloved; comforted as a child held on the lap of a parent.

Good Shepherd, come find me when I am lost.
Gather me to your heart when I am hurt.
Protect me when I am in harm's way.
I turn to you with gratitude for your tender love.

Do Not Fear

■ **Say to those who are of a fearful heart, Be strong, do not fear! Here is your God.** Isaiah 35:4

*I*saiah spoke these words to the people who were returning home after many years of exile. Their comfortable home-life had been disrupted and torn apart when they went into exile. Now, they were being uprooted once more in order to go home. Isaiah wanted them to remember that God was with them in their unsettledness.

The same kind of thing can happen to us emotionally or spiritually. Just when it seems we are settled for a while, life can bring upsetting or distressful situations. During these times our fears and anxieties easily come pushing through our calm and peace. We may be faith-filled persons, but our worries can pursue us relentlessly and destroy our sense of well-being.

The prophet Isaiah knew this. He encouraged those who were frightened and dismayed to believe that God was coming into their midst with strength and power. God would dispel their deep fears and concerns if they would only be open and would trust. Today's Advent Scripture reminds us, "Here is your God." Do our fears keep us from trusting God with our lives?

Trusted Companion,
I bring my fears and insecurities to you.
You are with me. I need not worry or be afraid.
Your shelter will be enough for me.

The Wisdom of Elizabeth

■ **Blessed is she who believed that there would be a fulfillment of what was spoken to her by the Lord.** Luke 1:45

*E*lizabeth was a wise woman, not only because of her age, but because of the way she perceived life. Her wisdom is evident in her greeting to Mary. Elizabeth knew there was a deeper message for her when she felt the baby kicking in her womb. She was caught up in the wonder of Mary's pregnancy. Elizabeth recognized the power of Mary's visit and how faithful God was. It was a moment of awe and joy as she exclaimed how fully God was present with them.

As Christmas draws near, it is easy to forget God's nearness as we rush around with many last-minute preparations. We need to slow down and catch Elizabeth's wisdom. She experienced a special moment and recognized it as an opportunity to sense God's nearness. She knew how much strength and comfort there was in that awareness. That's what led her to trust so strongly and to love so deeply. Let us look for signs of God's nearness as we complete Christmas preparations and enter into the joy of the season.

You continually make yourself present to me,
faithful and loving God.
I will slow down so I can recognize your presence
and celebrate the many ways you are with me.

A Tender Welcoming Home

■ . . . with great tenderness I will take you back . . . says the Lord, your redeemer. Isaiah 54:7-8 *(New American Bible)*

What a beautiful description Isaiah gives to God's welcoming us back after we have strayed. God does not just say rather grudgingly, "Oh, well, come on then, I guess I'll have to take you back. You're here and you look quite sorry for what you have done." No, Isaiah says it's not like that. God is ready to embrace us with great tenderness. Tenderness implies an affection for us. God is actually very fond of us and wonderfully delighted when we return from our reckless or wayward ways.

I wonder how most of us are in welcoming others when they have let us down, deliberately hurt us or refused to return our love. I wonder how much "great tenderness" is in our hearts when someone says, "I'd like a second chance. I blew it," or "I don't know what I was doing. I really made a mess of things. I know I've hurt you." Does our fondness and affection outweigh the pain and resentment in our hearts?

This Advent day let us remember that our God takes us back with great tenderness. Then let us renew our intention to welcome back others in the same way.

> *God of tenderness,*
> *thank you for the wide embrace of your welcome.*
> *How grateful I am that you do not hold grudges.*
> *How blessed I am that you always take me back.*

May the Light Shine Through Me

■ . . . the very works that I am doing, testify on my behalf that the Father has sent me. John 5:36

Jesus sent the messengers back to tell John the Baptist to trust what he had seen and heard, to believe the testimony of the works Jesus had done. Instead of giving John a huge theological answer to his questions, Jesus simply said, "Look at my life. What do you see there?" Similarly, my testimony to faith and values doesn't have to be given in eloquent and spacious answers. Rather, I need to live my life in such a way that it speaks about how much I believe in Jesus and his message.

In trying to have my life be the message, I have prayed these words of Cardinal John Newman each day for many years: "Jesus, shine through me and be so in me that every person I come in contact with may feel your presence in my soul." I yearn to have my life give this kind of testimony to God's goodness. It is not always easy to do and I fail often. But I have the comfort of knowing that the Light within me is always there, ready to be evidence of the Sacred Presence. As Christmas draws nearer, let us remember that it is who we are and what we do that truly testifies to the goodness of God.

Jesus, you call me to follow you.
I desire my life to give testimony to you
and to the power of your teachings.
Please guide me this day.

Making Room for God's Love

■ **Lift up, O gates, your lintels;
reach up, you ancient portals,
that the king of glory may come in.** Psalm 24:7
(New American Bible)

*L*intels or portals, probably the doorways of the temple, are pictured as too low for the King of glory to enter. The psalmist wants to emphasize that the doors must be very big because God is so great. Through metaphor, the psalmist is encouraging us to make more room in our own hearts for the magnitude of God's love to enter. God's entrance needs much openness. It is the expansive heart that has a large doorway of welcome, the big heart that has an entrance through which God's grace can easily move.

The busyness and pressure of the last days before Christmas sometimes leave hearts feeling anything but expansive and open. Fatigue and stress have often left me feeling grumpy and distraught, with harsh words and nasty judgments waiting to leap out of my mouth. The doorway to my heart at those times is very tiny. Christmas draws near. It is time to check the size of our heart-door and see if it needs some expanding to let the God of glory enter in.

*Gateway to Heaven,
your love is wide and deep.
May the doorway of my heart
always be large enough to welcome you.
Come enter in.*

Humming Your Praise and Joy

■ **My soul magnifies the Lord, and my spirit rejoices in God my Savior.** Luke 1:46-47

*H*ave you ever found yourself humming along when you are happy? Do you ever sing a little ditty as you are driving the car or working around the house or taking a shower? At times like these, the melody of a song is a spontaneous eruption of the human spirit, a way of expressing the satisfaction one feels.

Mary, mother of Jesus, and Hannah, mother of Samuel, had much to sing about—both had been surprised with the wondrous children of their wombs. Both marveled in song at how their lives had been filled with unexpected treasure. Because they were women of faith, both recognized that God was the source of their blessings. I can just hear these two women humming along as they went about their daily tasks.

As Christmas nears and so much emphasis is placed on material treasures, let us also look at our spiritual treasures and take time to proclaim the goodness of God in us. Today, choose a few lines of a favorite song or create a few lines of praise and thanksgiving to God. Hum or sing this melody as you go about your day. Praise God for all the goodness that is yours.

> *I take delight in you, my God.*
> *I sing a song of joy in my soul.*
> *I proclaim the wonder of your love*
> *through my words and actions.*

Light Dawns Upon Us

■ **By the tender mercy of our God, the dawn from on high will break upon us, to give light to those who sit in darkness and in the shadow of death, to guide our feet into the way of peace.** Luke 1:78-79

On this day before the feast of Christmas, we hear Zechariah's familiar canticle telling us that the dawn from on high will break upon us. Zechariah knew about darkness. He sat through nine months of it, unable to speak. He also knew about light, experiencing the power of Divine revelation when he prophesied through his canticle.

As we approach the celebration of the birth of Jesus, we are being invited to look within our own selves and within our world. Always we find some darkness there, mixed in with the light. It is to these dark corners that the Savior comes, bringing light by the tender mercy of God.

To the darkness of our hurrying, our self-centeredness, our weakness, our frustration, our half-lived lives, the Savior comes. To the darkness of our world of war and torture, alienation and deceit, greed and corruption, our Savior comes. The Light yearns to dawn upon us; we have only to open our hearts to receive this gift of loving presence.

Emmanuel, may your light
be perceived by all who sit in darkness.
Be a beacon of hope for all
whose lives are troubled this Christmas.

Beautiful Are They Who Bring Love

■ **How beautiful upon the mountains are the feet of the messenger who . . . brings good news.** Isaiah 52:7

*I*t is Christmas! It is the most wondrous feast—the birthday of the One who came to show us a God of love. How beautiful are the feet of those who walk the extra step across a room to greet someone with whom they have had differences. How beautiful are the feet of those who step beyond the material gifts and appreciate the heart of the giver. How beautiful are the feet of those who move about in the kitchen making the special foods and serving the guests who gather. How beautiful are the feet of those who not only go to church services but who also fully participate by greeting others joyfully, praying and singing heartily. How beautiful are the feet of those who walk into homeless shelters or places with little comfort to bring some of their own abundance.

Yes, how beautiful are all those feet who walk with glad tidings this day, with the intention of love in their hearts, for they are living the message of the One who came so long ago. The Christ of abundant love, born some two thousand years ago, lives on in us. As our feet take us near and far, let us continue to be the Christ to one another.

Divine Messenger,
I will carry the glad tidings
of your abundant and abiding love
to all I meet and greet today.

Held in God's Loving Hand

■ **You shall be a crown of beauty in the hand of the Lord, and a royal diadem in the hand of your God.** Isaiah 62:3

*T*his beautiful image of a diadem, a band of jewels placed on the head of royalty, describes the radical transformation that awaits the people of God as those who were exiled came home. Once treated as outcasts, now they would be precious gems, protected in the hand of God.

The Church chooses this passage from Isaiah for a Christmas reading in order to proclaim the deep and radical change that the coming of Jesus brought. He lived and taught compassionate, merciful love. He saw each person as a precious jewel. Jesus assured them that their lives would have the capability of being transformed.

What a wonderful way to think of ourselves this Christmas: as jewels in a circle of resplendent beauty, held in the protective and loving hand of God. As we look at the sparkling Christmas tree lights and dazzling ornaments, let us also look deep and find our spiritual jewels: the Spirit of Jesus within and among us, the love of family and friends, and the virtues and loving qualities we possess.

Resplendent Beauty,
thank you for coming to dwell among us
and for teaching us about our shining goodness.
I will remember that I am a jewel of love
in your royal crown of beauty.

The Many Songs of Christmas Day

■ **Make a joyful noise to the Lord, all the earth; break forth into joyous song and sing praises.** Psalm 98:4

Although Christmas hymns and carols fill the air with joy and gladness, not everyone will have a song of happiness in his or her heart today. Look around you at home, at church, at any gatherings you may attend today: what "songs" do you hear within others? Some may have a dirge in their hearts due to a recent death. Listen to their sorrow. Some may have an angry, wild rap song in their hearts. Be patient. Some may have the blues playing, brought on by relationship difficulties. Give them your understanding. Some may have an opera of their life's unending pain. Do not give up on them.

Look into your own heart. What is the song within you? Do you feel like singing? Can you catch any of the joy and happiness the Word-made-flesh has brought into our world? Be open to your own experience of God today. Do not deny your emptiness. Do not refuse your joy. Welcome the Christ within you in whatever form of song your heart bears.

Song of my Heart,
you came to dwell among us
as a source of great love.
May my heart resonate with your love
as I greet myself and others this day.

Seeing the Special in the Simple

■ . . . what we have heard, what we have seen with our eyes, what we have looked at and touched with our hands, concerning the word of life. 1 John 1:1

*J*ohn the apostle describes with awe how close he had been to the Word of life. His words remind me of a poem by Tagore in which he tells how he searched for many years, going to see high mountains and oceans, travelling everywhere to find God. Finally, after this intense and long search, Tagore writes, "I had not seen at my very doorstep, the dewdrop glistening on the ear of corn." Ah! How ordinary is our God-encounter, right at one's own doorstep in something as simple as a dewdrop on a plain vegetable.

I don't know about you, but something in me hesitates to trust revelations of God when they are too ordinary. I like to think that God is mostly revealed in something "big" or outstandingly beautiful, like the Swiss Alps. The truth is, however, that God is being revealed to us every day in those nearest to us, wherever we are. It is *how* we look for God, what we expect, that makes the difference. Let us give up the "high mountains and vast oceans" as our major searching places and come home to our simple lives.

> *I look for you today, God.*
> *What will I see and hear? What will I think?*
> *Whom will I touch? How will I feel?*
> *Will I encounter you in my ordinary day?*

Tears for the Children

■ "A voice was heard in Ramah, wailing and loud lamentation, Rachel weeping for her children . . ." Matthew 2:18

Can you imagine how your relatives or friends would have responded had you sent them a Christmas card with Rachel sobbing and lamenting for her children? They might have wondered why you were not caught up in the joy of the season or if perhaps you had missed the message of Christmas. But the Church asks us to reflect on the painful event of the Holy Innocents on a day near to the Nativity because it *is* a part of the "Christmas story." Jesus was a refugee very early in his life. The terrors of greed and unjust power affected his life when he was very young.

In every corner of the world today, there is a Rachel weeping for her children. These are the children who are victims of abuse, drugs, neglect, hunger, disease and poverty. We cannot ignore these children if we are truly welcoming Christ into our hearts. Indeed, it is an especially appropriate time to ponder how the Light of the World can work through us to change the pain and suffering of such children. Let us look for ways to comfort and care for them. Let us do our part to change the systems that perpetuate unjust and painful situations for children.

Mother of the little ones,
I bring you all neglected and hurt children.
Gather them to your compassionate bosom.
I promise to do my part to help
these beloved ones. Keep urging me to do so.

The Spirit's Power

■ . . . God anointed Jesus of Nazareth with the Holy Spirit and power. Acts 10:38

What was it like for Jesus when John baptized him? When he heard the voice from the heavens call him "the beloved"? He must have felt a surge of tenderness wash over him. A strong, assuring conviction of his relationship with God must have become firmly stored in his soul at that time. Jesus felt this power again and again in his life as he came forth from the desert, as he healed the sick, as he spent the nights alone in prayer, as he stood up for his beliefs, as he communed with his friends, as he walked the road to Calvary.

I have felt the effects of my own baptism time and again. I am surprised every time it happens. I notice this inner power when people tell me how much my words or actions helped them, or when I am hiking in the woods and, suddenly, I sense and pay attention to a presence much bigger than my own. I experience this power when I feel a nudge inside of me to be a better person or to do something to help alleviate the pain of my world. It is a wonderful gift, this power of the Holy Spirit. I invite you today to reflect on your own life and how you have experienced this potent presence of God.

Holy Spirit, I celebrate your life in me.
Your power filled me at my baptism
and continues to stir within me today.
Increase my awareness of this power for good
that daily lives within me.

Lent

A Call to Return
Ash Wednesday

■ **Return to the Lord, your God, for he is gracious and merciful, slow to anger, and abounding in steadfast love, and relents from punishing.** Joel 2:13

I am always amazed at how many people come to Ash Wednesday services. Each Lent I wonder what brings them there. Why do they make such an effort to take their lunch hour or to rise earlier than usual or to come to church after a wearying day's work when they might not come to Mass any other weekday of the year?

Perhaps it is the call to "return." Maybe a sense of hope is kindled in hearts by the possibility of coming back to God and trying once more to strengthen one's faith. I think it may also be the realization that there is always a part of one's heart that has not yet been given over to God. When we look within, we see that there is still more that needs to be brought home to the Holy One. There are always parts of us that we hold back and that need to be re-joined to God, in whose heart we truly belong.

This first day of Lent the Scriptures reassure us that God is rich in faithful love and waiting to welcome us home. Let us enter this Church season trusting that God will draw near and help us in our desire to "return."

> *I am re-turning to you, Friend of my heart.*
> *I am grateful that I belong to you*
> *and that you are always ready to welcome me home.*

Cleaning Out the Stale Air

■ . . . we urge you also not to accept the grace of God in vain.
2 Corinthians 6:1

Often at the end of Lent I feel as though I have missed many graced opportunities for spiritual growth. I usually end up losing my focus during Lent because I get much too preoccupied with being busy and with doing things that I think are important. But what could be more valuable than God's grace? That is why I usually feel a sense of freshness when Lent arrives. It's like a window inside me is being opened so the wind can come sweeping into the house and clean out the stale air. It is another opportunity to be intent on receiving God's grace.

I envision God's grace as being a generous, energizing movement of total Goodness. This stream of love is always available to each one of us. It is free and it is powerful. Grace can change our lives. All that we need do is be open to receiving it and attentive to Goodness in our daily lives. This Lent, let us pause each morning when we rise, stretch our arms wide and pray:

God of love, I open myself to you.
May I be aware of your powerful goodness,
given to me at every moment of this day.
May all I am and all I do bless others today.

The Courage to Change Heart

■ . . . if you offer your food to the hungry and satisfy the needs of the afflicted, then your light shall rise in the darkness and your gloom be like the noonday. Isaiah 58:10

A newspaper photo challenged me greatly: an eighteen-year-old black woman was using her body to shield a white Ku Klux Klan member who had fallen to the ground during a riot. He was being beaten by anti-Klan demonstrators. What an act of compassion! This woman, whose color and ethnicity are the KKK's target of cruel prejudice, risked being beaten herself to protect her enemy.

As I looked at the photo, I wondered if I would ever have the love and courage to do something like that. This young woman could have stood on the sidelines cheering to see her enemies being battered. Instead, she ran into the danger and tried to protect another human being from harm.

Lent is here and the passage from Isaiah reminds me that I have much changing of heart to do. Christianity is about much more than an easy handout; it is about making a commitment, and possibly paying dearly for it. Jesus gave us an example of such a commitment. Will we follow in his Way?

Strengthen my courage today, God of compassion,
to act out of love toward both friends and enemies,
even if it might cost me dearly.

Holding Fast to God

■ **Choose life so that you and your descendants may live, loving the Lord your God, obeying him, and holding fast to him.** Deuteronomy 30:19-20

Not long ago I was paying my weekly visit to the nearby hospice where I went to see Anna, a 93-year-old woman who was dying. What a striking image she presented as I walked into the room. She was a tall woman with long grey hair, and high, strong cheekbones. As I came near the bed, I couldn't believe my eyes: she was lying on her back, her long, thin right arm holding a small stuffed lamb close to her breast. She looked so secure and peaceful as she was nearing death. It truly was a beautiful image of "holding fast."

When we hold fast to God we are choosing not to be separated from the One who embraces us with love and compassion. Holding fast to God is easiest for me when I let go of my desire to control all of life myself, hardest when I feel emotionally drained and distant from my inner Source.

What about you? What does it mean to "hold fast to God," and when is it easier or more difficult for you? Lent is a good time for all of us to recommit ourselves to holding fast to God.

Embrace me, Enduring Love.
I hold fast to you with a trusting heart,
ready to heed your voice
and to rest in your care.

My Heart Needs Some Cleansing

■ **Create in me a clean heart, O God, and put a new and right spirit within me.** Psalm 51:10

*E*very once in a while, my heart needs to be cleansed, rinsed off, revived and renewed. As dirt and grime on a window pane make it dull and opaque, so does my inner vision become cloudy. I regularly need to notice what I do and do not see when I look from my heart's perspective.

What are some of the things that collect and need to be cleaned off the windowpane of my heart? I often need to brush off frantic busyness so I can see God more clearly in people and events. Harsh thoughts and hasty judgments must be washed away. The residue from old battles with others needs to be rinsed off. I have to cleanse my heart of anxiety and lack of trust. Racism must be scrubbed off. On and on the list goes.

Time for reflection and prayer is vital in order to keep my inner transparency. If I am too busy or too preoccupied with the external details of life, I can often miss what needs cleansing in my heart.

Loving God, bathe me in your mercy.
Clear my inner windowpane.
Help me to see with your merciful eyes,
to love with your incredible love.

Take Hold of God's Strong Hand

■ **The Lord brought us out of Egypt with a mighty hand and an outstretched arm . . .** Deuteronomy 26:8

When did you last notice your hands? Take a look at them now. Think of all the things that your hands do. Notice how they hold this booklet, how you can turn pages with them, lift yourself from the chair . . . Hands are wonderful gifts. What a difficult life it would be without hands. We easily take our hands for granted, until they become arthritic or succumb to some other physical ailment.

Not surprisingly, Scripture records the "mighty hand" of God freeing the Israelites. The hand of God is an apt metaphor for the strength of divine grace and the assurance of divine guidance. The Israelites had only to put their hand in the hand of God as they crossed the wilderness into the Promised Land. We know, however, that they often failed to do this. They were too preoccupied with their own agenda and did not recognize the "mighty hand" of God when it was held out to them. In our journey to the Promised Land, we are also offered the "mighty hand" of God to guide and console us. May we open ourselves to receive this divine strength and guidance.

God of courage,
today I place my hand in your hand.
As I journey through Lent,
I will trust in your guidance.

Do I Seek Quick Fixes?

■ This generation is an evil generation; it asks for a sign, but no sign will be given to it except the sign of Jonah.

Luke 11:29

*T*hose who surrounded Jesus were enthralled with miraculous healings. They were not nearly so immersed in the call to spiritual conversion that Jesus taught. In this passage, Jesus is irritated that the people only wanted quick fixes and instant healing. They didn't want to hear about the slow process of changing their hearts. So Jesus said they would only receive the "sign of Jonah," the sign of conversion.

I realize that I could also be like those people who eagerly sought "signs." I want my life to go well, to not have any glitches or difficulties. I still seek "miracles." That is why I need constantly to ask myself these and many other similar questions: Do I pray more intently and eagerly for my life to be problem-free than I do for my ability to forgive someone who has wronged me? Do I put more energy into praying for a book to sell well than I do to be mindful of living each moment of my day with gratitude? Do I still expect God magically to cure my ills instead of trusting God to help me enter into those struggles so I can grow and change as I experience them?

Jesus, you call me to conversion.
Help me to let go of my need for "signs"
and to be more intent on changing my heart.

In All the Familiar Places

■ **"Come," my heart says, "seek his face!" Your face, Lord, do I seek.** Psalm 27:8

I came home from the supermarket recently feeling miffed because I couldn't find my favorite frozen yogurt. A few weeks later as I looked in the frozen food section, behold, there it was, only in a completely different-looking container. That's why I hadn't found it before.

When I think of seeking God, the same sort of thing occurs. I can be looking for God in the people and places where I have always discovered the divine presence and miss God completely in a new container. It is easy to seek God in the bliss of peaceful relationships, the comfort of the sacraments, and the joy of successful living. If I only look for God in the good things of my life, I will miss many facets of this loving presence. I need to focus on the unwanted, the uncomfortable, and the unexpected parts of my life.

This Lent we can ask ourselves: Do I look for God's presence in the angry driver yelling obscenities, in the physician who misdiagnosed a critical illness, in the jailed drug dealer, in the uncooperative neighbor who makes life miserable for others, in the child who lies and cheats, in the politician who has opposing views, in the family member who shuns me?

Open my heart, God,
so I see you everywhere today.
I know it is easy to miss you
so I will look very closely.

Plotting Against Others

■ Then they said, "Come, let us make plots against Jeremiah."
Jeremiah 18:18

The people began to plot against Jeremiah because his message disrupted their neat, secure world even though that world was filled with injustice. They tried to figure out how to get rid of him so his words would not worry them or prick their consciences. People also plotted against Jesus. They wanted to destroy him because he, too, challenged their complacent lives.

"Plotting" often involves the human voice: talking, gossiping, urging, whispering and being secretive, analyzing, manipulating, and hiding the real truth in order to make things go the way one wants them to go. During Lent we might consider who we want to change and how we use our voice to try to make that happen. Who gets in our way or tends to disrupt our neat and tidy world? What do we secretly wish on them? Do we try to "get rid" of them? Do we seek their downfall, or try to put them in their place, or force them to come over to our way of thinking? Do we connive and get others to help us by backbiting, half-truths, spreading rumors or lies?

I will need help today, God,
to watch my mind and my mouth,
to notice what I say and why I say it.
May I speak with kindness and integrity.

Time to Yield and Trust

■ **When you grow old, you will stretch out your hands, and someone else will fasten a belt around you and take you where you do not wish to go.** John 21:18

I was recently at the bedside of a 45-year-old woman who was dying of cancer. Her 70-year-old father was there feeding her. It was a touching scene. With her bald head and her inability to feed herself, she might well have looked like the baby he fed long ago. I thought of how much we all want to control our lives, to be "in charge." Yet there are times when life does not go as we want, when all we can do is yield and trust God with the difficult process.

Jesus used the metaphor of surrender to speak with Peter about his controlling ways. It was Peter who was always sure that he knew what was best, jumping out of the boat to walk on the lake, then promptly falling in the water as his faith faltered. It was Peter who hastily chopped off an ear of the high priest's servant, thinking that was what Jesus needed. It was Peter who quickly said he'd follow Jesus anywhere but then denied him just as swiftly. Like Peter, we think we know what is best but we forget the help and guidance we need from God.

When I want to be too controlling,
wake me up, God.
Remind me to surrender
and to be led by you.

Someone Needs My "Scraps"

■ **And at his gate lay a poor man named Lazarus, covered with sores, who longed to satisfy his hunger with the scraps that fell from the rich man's table . . .** Luke 16:20-21

Many of us are, in a way, like the rich man: "rich" in good health, in free time, in faith, in friendship, in courage, in enthusiasm, or anything we have abundantly. Every day someone comes and begs at our table. They may not say anything aloud, but their presence tells us they would gladly eat from the scraps that fall from our table of life.

What might our scraps be? Someone who is depressed may need to feast on our patience while we wait with them to recover. Someone homebound or unable to care well for themselves may want to be fed with the gift of our time in a visit or phone call or home-cooked meal. Someone who lacks self-esteem or has had a serious failure may be grateful for our words of affirmation. All the "someones" of our world come to our table of faith and would gladly partake of the riches of our prayer.

At times we are the poor ones at the table. I recall a time when I felt very unhappy with myself and an unknown person gave me a wonderful smile. That smile was the most delicious scrap of nourishment!

Gift-giving God,
let me recognize my riches
and generously share what I have
with those in need.

Wash Me From My Guilt

■ **Wash me thoroughly from my iniquity, and cleanse me from my sin.** Psalm 51:2

Notice that the psalmist did not just pray "cleanse me from my sin," but also included "wash me thoroughly from my iniquity." It is so human to hold onto guilt even after we have come to terms with our sin and asked for forgiveness and mercy. We can feel guilty for years over something we have actually done, or thought we might possibly have done. We can blame ourselves and obsess over what wretches we are, but all that this guilt does is dig us further into the hole of self-deprecation.

Obsessive guilt is not the message that the Scriptures offer to us. Think of those powerful stories of the prodigal son, the good thief on the cross, or the woman caught in adultery. Over and over we are assured that God is forgiving and that we have only to come with a contrite heart and we will be washed clean from our past failures. "Being washed clean" means that there is a fresh, new start without the residue from the past. God offers us a new beginning. The problem is that too often we think God couldn't possibly forgive us for this or that thing we did. We doubt the generosity of God's heart.

O God, I long to absorb fully
your all-cleansing love.
Open my heart to accept the fresh beginning
that your merciful love offers me.

Invite God Into Your Life

■ **Knock, and the door will be opened for you.** Matthew 7:7

Doors are a favorite image of mine because they can represent so many facets of the spiritual life. Doors can be opened or closed, they can welcome or shut out, allow an entrance to or an exit from a place. Jesus once referred to himself as a door or a gate. No wonder he used the door as an image when he was encouraging trust and hope in his listeners' hearts.

When I am in situations that are difficult, frustrating or confusing, I often hear God saying to me: "Don't rely only on yourself. I will come into your life if you will invite and welcome me there. The two of us together can do much more for this situation than just you, by yourself. Trust me to be there for you."

When I finally get beyond my independence and knock on the divine door, it opens quickly and I wonder, "Why didn't I do this sooner? Why didn't I pray about this before now? Why did I think I could work this through without any divine guidance? What kept me from going to the Source of strength and wisdom?" It's not that I always get what I want when I knock on that divine door but I can always count on receiving what I need. It's just a matter of trust.

Door of Life,
I hand over all my cares to you.
I know that you are always ready
to listen, to comfort and to guide me.

The Courage to Speak the Truth

■ **The Lord heard her cry. Just as she was being led off to execution, God stirred up the holy spirit of a young lad named Daniel . . .** Daniel 13:44-45

This story about lust and deceit is also about bringing harm to others by judging them without knowing the facts. Suzanna seemed doomed. The two lustful elders thought they had cleverly taken care of all the loopholes in their story and that Suzanna's truth would never be discovered. However, they had not considered the power of God to move the heart of Daniel. He challenged those who condemned her to have a fair trial that finally brought out the truth.

Isn't it amazing how one person's false statement can condemn and how another's true statement can save? Like the people who were quick to judge Suzanna, we, too, can quickly condemn another by believing damaging hearsay and repeating it. One false statement of ours can ruin a reputation. Equally true, one affirming statement of ours, spoken with courage and daring, can heal a person's life.

Spirit of Life, stir within me today.
Grant me courage to speak the truth when it is needed
and to keep silent when my words would harm another.

Listen to Your Hunger for God

■ **Such fasting as you do today will not make your voice heard on high.** Isaiah 58:4

*T*he prophet Isaiah challenged the people who fasted for the wrong reasons, those for whom fasting was simply obeying the letter of the law without affecting their relationship with God. Fasting can be a means of significant spiritual growth, but so much depends on *why* we do it.

What are some good motivations for fasting? One is to remember God's nearness. I get so busy that I lose my sense of God's presence sometimes. When I am hungry, there is an "a-ha" within that reminds me: "Listen to your hunger for God." Other times, I am too self-oriented, so I fast to deepen my awareness of my sisters and brothers who lack adequate food and drink. And sometimes I let fasting slow me down when I am zooming along too quickly. With less food, I eat slowly and savor more fully.

I encourage you this Lent to think about why you fast and to consider what you most need for spiritual growth. Perhaps each time you fast, it may be for a slightly different reason. Whatever you do, let your fasting draw you to the heart of God.

I yearn for you, my divine Companion.
I hunger for your spiritual food
to strengthen my faith.
I thirst for your truth to set me free.

Little Things Can Change Us

■ . . . **if the prophet had commanded you to do something extraordinary, would you not have done it?** 2 Kings 5:13

Why is it so difficult to believe that God can do marvelous things through the most ordinary circumstances? Why does it often take a big catastrophic event before we are finally convinced of what we need for our spiritual transformation? I recently read the story of survivors of a plane crash ten years ago. A flight attendant and a nurse both elaborated on how they had changed and are now firmly established in a relationship with God. I wondered how many people reading the newspaper would be even further convinced that it takes something big before we turn our lives around.

Lent is a good time to find our spiritual transformation through the ordinary, humdrum of everyday life, for there most spiritual changes happen. Most of us won't experience something like a plane crash or major accident. If, like Naaman, we expect that the "little stuff" is of no importance or value, then we may miss the very opportunities where God is calling us and inviting us to change our hearts. Be aware today of little things.

Transforming God,
keep wooing me in the midst of my ordinary life.
Focus my attention on the little things
that challenge me and call me to you.

Balancing Independence and Community

■ **Do not think that I have come to abolish the law or the prophets . . .** Matthew 5:17

*J*esus had a healthy respect for the law, seeing what needed to be changed and what was vital for following his teachings. I learned this the hard way in my early years in religious community. I had reached a point in my life when I felt I needed a change in ministry. So I did what I thought was a very positive thing: I went away for several days and prayed about it. When I returned, I went to the sister who was then my superior and told her what I had decided. I will never forget her response: "And why do you think you can decide all by yourself what is good for you and for the community?"

That may seem harsh, but I needed to hear it, being a very independent person who liked to make decisions on her own. Praying about it alone was good, but she was right: I needed to check it out with the community to see if it was good for all involved. That is what good law does for us. It allows us to know our own needs and to make good decisions, always with an openness and a sense of how it will affect the whole community.

Ruler and Guide, I will respect your law.
I will align my ways with your ways
while I keep in mind the needs of others.

God's Passionate Love for Us

■ **I will heal their disloyalty;
I will love them freely . . .** Hosea 14:4

Do we ever fully realize how amazing the love of God is for us? No matter how seared, smudged and stained our life may be, we will always be received into the merciful embrace of God when we choose to return. Sometimes I think we use the phrase "God loves you" so often that it becomes a bland saying that lies limply in the air, having little effect on those who hear it.

To be loved freely by God, as Hosea states, is a tremendous thing. It is to be received without doubt or hesitation, to be always regarded as a beloved and cherished one. At a recent retreat, my co-facilitator and I carried around a mirror to each retreatant as part of the closing. We held it in front of each one and said to her, "May you always know that God is crazy about you."

This blessing was our way of emphasizing the truth and beauty of God's passionate love for us. I suggest you try it today. First, think of your failings, mistakes, sins. Then go stand in front of the mirror. Look fully into your eyes and say, "God is crazy about you." Keep returning to the mirror until you believe it.

Passionate God, you are wildly in love with me.
You are ecstatic about the wonder of my being.
Keep trying to convince me of this immense truth.
I will keep trying to believe it.

Growing in Spiritual Freedom

■ **And Joshua said to all the people, "Thus says the Lord, the God of Israel . . ."** Joshua 24:2

Joshua retells the well-known story of God's deliverance of the Israelites from the land of Egypt, their place of slavery. He tells this story, and other tales of victory, to remind the people of how faithful and generous God has been to them throughout the ages. In Joshua's recountings, God always delivers the people out of the hands of their enemies.

In our own personal histories, God is constantly inviting us to move out of the land of our enslavements and bondage. If we look back on our lives, we can see how God has been our guide to greater spiritual freedom. There have been many graced moments, and God continues to lead us out of whatever keeps us from being our true selves. We are constantly guided by God to be more loving people of integrity and goodness.

Today, let us look back and recall how we have grown with God's guidance. As we remember these graced moments, let us give thanks.

> *Spirit of God,*
> *deliver me out of the hands of my enemies.*
> *Lead me to greater spiritual freedom*
> *as I become more fully my true self.*

For Mercy's Sake

■ **But if you had known what this means, "I desire mercy and not sacrifice," you would not have condemned the guiltless.** Matthew 12:7

*J*esus and his disciples were walking through a field of grain. The Pharisees became upset when the hungry disciples pulled off and ate some of the heads of grain because such activity was not permitted on the Sabbath. Jesus responded to their criticism by telling the Pharisees that he was not so concerned about the rules of the law (sacrifice) as he was about the way people related to one another (mercy).

I know Jesus' words are true for me: I'd rather fast for a day anytime (sacrifice) than have to be kind and open to someone who has dealt me a low blow (mercy). I would rather choose my own daily sacrifices than have them come to me in the form of critical people, impatient drivers, grumbling friends and irritable coworkers. How much easier it is to give up a piece of candy or go to church on Sunday than to stay loving toward those who mess up my day. Sacrifices I choose seem easy compared to the continual kindness required by Jesus.

Merciful God,
I will accept the difficult people of my day.
May the sacrifices I choose be ones
filled with love and kindheartedness.

Suffering: A Source of Inspiration

■ **Then he began to teach them that the Son of Man must undergo great suffering . . . and be killed, and after three days rise again.** Mark 8:31

When Jesus tried to explain to his disciples that he must "undergo great suffering," Peter would not hear of it. He couldn't bear the thought that his dear friend would have to go through such great pain. One can imagine Peter saying to Jesus, "Now just stop that kind of talk. Nothing terrible is going to happen to you." He denied the suffering that Jesus knew would happen.

Peter refused to accept the fact that suffering was a part of Jesus' journey. He did not understand that this suffering was to be a source of transformation. His response was very natural, very human. None of us wants the suffering that comes our way. But if we have faith to see it as a part of our own journey of transformation, it can be a grace-filled experience. Peter apparently did not hear, or did not understand, what Jesus said about rising from the dead. Perhaps if Peter had really heard this hopeful statement, he would not have been so quick to fight Jesus' journey of suffering.

Crucified One, help me to learn
from the suffering that is part of my life,
to not deny the possibility of my growing from it.

A God So Close

■ **For what other great nation has a god so near to it as the Lord our God is whenever we call . . . ?** Deuteronomy 4:7

*I*t can be very frustrating to keep calling someone on the phone and receive no answer, or to be a parent speaking to children who do not listen, or to call out to someone and have them turn away without responding. The author of Deuteronomy reminds us that this is not the way it is with our God who hears us whenever we call. God does not turn away or pretend not to hear. When we do not feel the Lord's presence, it may be difficult for us to believe that God is close by and always listening to us.

We simply have to trust God's promises. Again and again, the Scriptures assure us that God is near, that we will always be heard. One of my graced moments was when I read the chapter in Hannah Hunnard's *Hinds Feet on High Places* in which the Shepherd assures Much Afraid that she will never be alone on her journey. All she has to do is call and he will be there for her. As I look back on my life, I can honestly say that God has never let me down. Always I have been heard, in ways I never expected.

Good Shepherd,
encourage me to call upon you,
to trust that you will always be there
when I am in difficulty and distress.

I Need a Willing Spirit

■ **Restore to me the joy of your salvation, and sustain in me a willing spirit.** Psalm 51:12

Like the psalmist, I long to have a "willing spirit." I don't often think about having a will, but it is a precious gift. I once heard the will described as a "spiritual muscle." That seems to name it very well because every human has the ability to choose and to direct one's behavior and actions. Without a will we wouldn't do much. So why pray for a "willing spirit"? Well, I know that I can get "willful," stubborn, stuck in my own ways. Sometimes I'd rather do what I want to do, even when I know it is not for the best. God asks me to have a willing spirit, to be open, eager, ready to hear God's voice and follow God's ways. Yes, I do need to have a willing spirit sustained in me.

Today, let us make these beautiful words from Psalm 51 part of our prayer: sit quietly and begin to notice how your breath goes in and out. As you breathe in, pray: "Sustain in me." As you breathe out, pray: "A willing spirit." Repeat this pattern over and over until these words are a deep and resonating part of yourself. Take these words into the world with you today and be eager and ready to attend to God's bidding.

Spirit of God,
you have given me what I need
in order to make good choices.
May I be attentive to your voice today
and heed your call to follow your ways.

Feeling "Scabby"

■ **A new heart I will give you, and a new spirit I will put within you.** Ezekiel 36:26

$\mathcal{R}$eading a Thomas Merton journal recently, I smiled when I saw his description of a particular day: "It is one of those days when you feel scabby." I thought, "I know the feeling!" It's when we pick at ourselves, it's when we don't like that "protrusion" on our spiritual skin. "Feeling scabby" is often the time when I am getting in touch with the inner part of myself that I do not like, the parts that I want to have changed so I can be a more loving person. As soon as I recognize one of these unwanted aspects of myself, I want to get rid of it immediately.

As I thought about the constant need to have my heart renewed and the longing for God to continually place a new spirit within me, I realized that this longing is a great gift. If one is being faithful to prayer and the inner life, more and more layers of the deeper self will be peeled back and things that need changing will be revealed. If we do not want to change, we should not pray. Our weaknesses can lead to discouragement unless there is also a recognition of the transforming power of God. When we feel scabby, it is important to continue to love ourselves as God loves us, to keep welcoming ourselves home as God welcomes us.

> *Creator and Friend,*
> *today I will befriend my scabbiness.*
> *I will welcome my whole self,*
> *strengths and weaknesses,*
> *and not be discouraged by the growth*
> *that is yet to be mine.*

Divine Exasperation

■ **And [Jesus] sighed deeply in his spirit and said, "Why does this generation ask for a sign?"** Mark 8:12

*J*esus was exasperated because the Pharisees were testing him. He found it irritating when they asked for a sign. How Jesus must have longed for them to believe his message without asking him to prove it.

I rarely think of Jesus as the Exasperated One. Most often I see him as the Loving or Compassionate One. Yet to deny Jesus' exasperation is to deny Jesus a part of his humanity. There were times when Jesus was frustrated, irritated and upset. These emotional responses did not make him any less good or holy. Rather, his responses confirmed that he was fully human. Jesus continued to love and care for others even when he sighed deeply at their sin and failures.

That we are all capable of a great mix of emotions is something we should always keep in mind. We may be loved dearly by someone but also experience their irritability and exasperation at times, just as we can get upset with others whom we love. While it is essential to control our emotions in order to act lovingly, it is also necessary to accept these human responses of ours as quite natural.

Creator of my humanity,
help me to accept the unwanted emotions
that arise spontaneously within me.
I will be aware and not allow them
to keep me from being a loving person.

A Wholehearted Return

■ **Yet even now, says the Lord, return to me with all your heart . . .** Joel 2:12

*E*ach Lent I hear the phrase "return with *all* your heart"—and I gulp. Surrendering one's whole being to God is quite a challenge. Every Lent I look again into my heart to discover those places that have not yet returned to the One who calls me. This is the wisdom behind having a Lenten journey each year. Knowing that I will be re-invited to return to God keeps me from being discouraged as I struggle to give more of my whole self to this loving Creator.

What does it mean to "return"? Re-turning indicates that I have been there, that I am making a shift, turning around and heading there again. I cannot re-turn to a place where I have not already been. I find this thought very comforting because I know that if I go to the very depths of my being, I belong totally to God. Some places of my heart have strayed and lost their way, but I know they can return to God. Lent is a time to go looking for these places. Lent is also a time to remember that God's invitation stands forever. Always God waits for us to return with all our heart.

Thank you, loving God,
for the challenging invitation
to re-turn to you
with my entire being.

The Suffering Servant

■ **You are my servant . . . in whom I will be glorified.**
                                                      Isaiah 49:3

When a servant of God is suffering, he or she rarely knows what kind of growth will happen or how the glory of God will be made known. Jesus, the suffering Servant of God, experienced a journey of pain and sorrow. He accepted his passion and death as a part of his life's pattern of transformation. It is no different for his followers. This truth is at the heart of the Christian journey. Our lives will have pain, hurt, turmoil, frustration, and many other sufferings. These can be part of our growth, depending on our attitude.

We can meet the suffering in our life for unhealthy reasons, such as getting attention, feeding our discouragement, avoiding work or escaping relational conflicts or we can accept it in the manner of Jesus, as a part of life and an essential element for growth. In her book *I Dreamed of Africa*, Kuki Gallmann wrote to her son: " . . . learn the lesson of acceptance . . . as only through acceptance you will find the secret of existence . . . and you will use all that happens in your life, your joys and your sorrows to become a better person." If we simply fight suffering, it remains our enemy. If we befriend it and learn from it, we can eventually become more compassionate and understanding. This truth is at the heart of the Christian journey.

Suffering Servant, you are my mentor
as I experience pain and hurt in my own life.
Teach me through my sufferings.
Let me learn and grow through them.

Sometimes Dew Is Enough

■ **I will be like the dew to Israel . . .** Hosea 14:5

One of my fond memories of childhood on an Iowa farm is the dew of summer mornings. The coolness of a new dawn and the grass would be deliciously wet on my small bare feet. I remember my father speaking one time of how his corn crop could be saved in a dry season if there was enough heavy dew each day. This moisture on the leaves could be absorbed by the plant and would help it to survive.

God promises to be like dew for Israel. It is this dew which will help Israel to "blossom like a lily." This is a very significant promise because Israel was in a tough place, a dry summer—struggling with the sin of the people and with the terrors of enemies of the land. Undoubtedly, Israel wanted more than "dew." A nice, full rainfall of help would have been greatly welcomed, but the dew was enough to get Israel through to better times. Isn't that like our lives? Sometimes we are in a tough spot and all we have is a little dew. Yet, this bit of spiritual moisture or help from God is enough to see us through until better times.

> *Gentle Dew, falling into my life,*
> *I will welcome your spiritual moisture coming to me*
> *instead of bemoaning the lack of a great rainfall.*
> *Your little gifts of comfort and joy each day*
> *are enough to strengthen and encourage me.*

Learning to Trust

■ **Jesus said to him, "Go; your son will live." The man believed the word that Jesus spoke to him and started on his way.** John 4:50

*T*rusting the words of Jesus seems so natural in this story. I rarely find it so clear and simple. Usually, I am either unsure about what to do or I discount what might happen. I want certainty about the situation. Yet the direction for my life is usually not that precise or apparent. This Gospel story reminds me to listen closely to life because God speaks through people, events, and many situations besides my own meditation. I need to trust that God is with me. I am often not sure what I "hear" at first, so I need to be patient and to ponder it a while. I also have to trust my prayer, my intuition and the promises in Scripture which assure me of God's guidance.

I am always re-learning trust in God. One year I was searching for a place to live. I fretted and stewed. Finally, I just let go and stopped being anxious, placing my confidence in God. After this, a friend of mine unexpectedly helped me find a place that was much more wonderful than anything I had envisioned. How much worry and anxiety I could have avoided had I trusted God and believed much sooner that all would be well.

> *I will trust that you are with me, God.*
> *I believe that you will guide me.*
> *I place my confidence in you*
> *even when my faith is wobbly and unsure.*

When Anger Is Not Sinful

■ **But I say to you that if you are angry with a brother or sister, you will be liable to judgment . . .** Matthew 5:22

*M*uch has been written in recent years about anger. We now know that anger is an ordinary emotion which is essential for healthy human growth. Anger can provide necessary self-protection. It can help us to rise up in protest against injustice. When anger is withheld or pressed down inside a person, it can push back out again in violent or deviant behavior. So when is anger sinful? Or "liable to judgment"?

The answer lies in the command of Jesus to not hold grudges. It is not sinful to feel anger, but it is wrong to use this emotion to harm another, to harbor anger, to savor the taste of hatred, to feed on the resentment and bitterness which anger can bring. When we let our anger smolder and continue to nurture its raging flames by our thoughts and behavior, then anger can become a tool of violence rather than a help for our growth. Refusing to speak to another, spreading lies and gossip, willingly desiring pain and harm to others—these can all be ways which turn anger from a natural human emotion into an ugly, evil sore in our spirit.

Spirit of Wisdom, grant me a discerning mind
so I will know when my anger is for good
and when my anger is bringing harm.
Keep encouraging me to be reconciled
with those whom my anger has hurt or held apart.

Standing Near Those Who Suffer

■ **Though an army encamp against me, my heart shall not fear . . .** Psalm 27:3

As I read the Scripture bringing us into the days of Holy Week, I felt a deep sadness. I thought of Jesus and the profound aloneness and loneliness that was his during his final days as he went up to Jerusalem and on to Calvary. I pictured the disciples sleeping while Jesus agonized in the garden. I saw his followers fleeing and leaving him alone with the soldiers. I heard the greeting of betrayal by Judas and Peter's denial. And I looked to see only a handful of loved ones standing in compassion at the foot of his cross.

It is hard enough to go through pain and heartache when we have support and encouragement. How excruciating it is to feel abandoned or misunderstood or isolated when we are experiencing trials and tribulations. Holy Week is a call to join with Jesus in his lonely journey. Let us look at our world and see how we can give support and encouragement to those who are on their own Calvary journey of pain and sorrow.

Faithful God,
thank you for those who stood by me
when I was miserable with hurt and pain.
I promise to draw near with compassionate attention
to those needing my presence in their times of travail.

The Pain of Betrayal

■ . . . one of you will betray me. Matthew 26:21

One can easily abhor the treachery of Judas in selling Jesus to his enemies. Betrayal is one of the deepest hurts of the human heart. This is especially evident in marital infidelity and in the betrayal of children by adults who use or abuse them. How painful it is to be lied to, abandoned, deceived or abused by someone who was trusted.

When I look at my own life, I see that there are times when there is a Judas in me. This betrayer in me rears its wretched head when I do not live up to the values and ideals I proclaim. I can sell my beliefs and my dreams for very little when I am anxious, tired, fearful or hurt. I can toss around another's reputation for the price of a laugh or an unwarranted harsh judgment. I can sell my compassion for my own brief comfort.

I recall a meeting at which I sold my kindness and care for the price of my own convenience. An older woman was there who did not have a ride home, and I knew she would ask me for one because I lived in her direction. When the meeting ended, I quickly walked out so I would not hear her request and have to be inconvenienced by the extra time it would take. In that moment, I sold my strong belief in being a compassionate woman.

Beloved Christ, kissed on the cheek by Judas,
you knew the immense pain of being betrayed.
When I am tempted to sell out cheaply,
may I have the wisdom and the fortitude
to make a loving choice that reflects your love.

We Are Only
Passing Through

■ . . . you shall eat it hurriedly. It is the passover of the Lord.
Exodus 12:11

*T*he Passover celebration commemorated the Jewish deliverance from slavery. The blood of the slain lamb marked the
doorposts of those to be delivered. These households were
passed over by the angel of death. This event reminded the
people that God was with them and would never leave them.

In the first Passover the people are described as true pilgrims, standing as they ate, ready to leave instantly. On Holy
Thursday, Jesus celebrates a new Passover and gives the Bread
of Life as nourishment for our journey to spiritual freedom.
This celebration is an invitation to remember that we are
pilgrims on a spiritual journey in which God travels with us.

On Holy Thursday, let us remember that God is always
ready to nourish us on this journey to our true Homeland. We
are only passing through this time and place. While our life
here is valuable and essential to our spiritual growth, we
cannot get so rooted and attached to earthly values that we
refuse to hear the call of God to move on to deeper growth.
Today, let us partake of the Eucharist "like those who are in
flight," ready to go and eager to grow.

Pilgrim God,
loosen my tight hold
on whatever keeps me
from being free to grow.

A Time of Surrender

■ **When Jesus had received the wine, he said, "It is finished."
Then he bowed his head and gave up his spirit.** John 19:30

My friend Cathy found a sense of peace as she entered the hospital for cancer surgery. She had reached the point where there was no other choice but to surrender to whatever the results would be. She deliberately surrendered her life to God and gave her spirit over in trust. It was her moment of uniting with the Christ of Calvary, for Jesus, too, had his time of total surrender. He knew what it was like to let go completely.

It is not only at the moment of our death that we are asked to trust God with our lives. Day by day we must surrender our fears, worries, doubts and discouragement into the Holy One's hands, with complete hope that God will never forsake us, even though it may at times feel that way.

Think of what causes you the most anxiety, heartache and worry. This is your Calvary-connection, your call to surrender. Can you entrust that part of your life to God?

Jesus Crucified,
the final moment of your total surrender
teaches me how to let go with a trusting heart.
I can draw strength from you today.

Easter to Pentecost

A Model of Love and Devotion

■ **Early on the first day of the week, while it was still dark, Mary Magdalene came to the tomb . . .** John 20:1

*I*magine how early Mary had to get up to get to the tomb. Think of the courage it took to go in the predawn darkness. No street lights to guide her footsteps, no way to see any lurking dangers. It was probably no safer then than it is now for women to be walking alone in the dark. She was in a graveyard, not the most comfy place to be strolling. What love and dedication this woman had. How much she must have loved Jesus to risk doing what she did.

As I celebrate Easter this year, I look at all my lame excuses for not being more dedicated and loving in my relationships and in my work. I sometimes find myself whining about the littlest things like getting up early to pray, answering another phone call, packing my suitcase for the umpteenth time, etc. I forget that there is a price to be paid if one is to be a disciple of the Risen Christ. If I truly have the joy and fire of Easter in my spiritual bones, I will be willing to do such things as make an extra effort to have quality prayer, graciously do what is needed as part of my ministry, and give of my precious time for the sake of loving another.

Risen Jesus,
renew my zeal and dedication.
Restore my desire to serve with joy
and enliven my spiritual bones.

Stay With Me

■ **But they urged him strongly, saying, "Stay with us . . ." So he went in to stay with them.** Luke 24:29

*T*his segment of the Emmaus story is very poignant. The disciples had been downcast, disheartened. Life seemed dismal, gloomy. Then they met Jesus on the road and he opened their hearts. When the time came for the evening meal, they felt a strong bond with this "stranger." The pain of their hearts was eased, and he filled them with hope.

As we remember the presence of the Risen Christ this week, we, too, can beg him to stay with us. It is a good time to reflect on where we most need the love, the guidance, the encouragement of Jesus now. Is there any place where we are trying to "go it alone"? Do we have decisions to make where inviting Jesus to be with us would help us find the direction we seek? As we awake each morning, do we consciously ask Jesus to be with us? After prayer, do we invite him to stay with us all the day? Before sleep, do we pray, "Stay with me through the night"? When we urge Jesus to "stay with us," it reminds us of how near the Risen Christ is to us and it affirms our deep belief that we need this presence in our life.

Where do you especially need the Risen Christ? Invite him to stay with you there.

Risen One,
there are places in my life
where I especially need you.
Come and stay with me.

Even Entombed, We Aren't Alone

■ **I shall not die, but I shall live, and recount the deeds of the Lord.** Psalm 118:17

*L*ast year during Lent someone sent me a postcard with a print of the 14th Station of the Cross by the American Southwest artist De Grazia. It shows the body of Jesus bound in white cloths lying upon a slab of concrete. Completely surrounding the body are many angels, little, soft, rounded, brightly colored figures with heads bowed in sadness. I carried that print around with me for weeks, feeling a bond with it that I could not understand. It was several weeks after Easter before I caught the message for myself.

The De Grazia print is a powerful portrayal of hope and comfort. Jesus is in the tomb of darkness, just as we often are in our own tombs of darkness. He is surrounded by these beautiful, compassionate figures depicting love and care. He is not abandoned in his tomb time—and neither are we. We may feel desolate and despairing when our lives are filled with death and tomb-like situations, but we, too, are surrounded with God's compassionate love. God will "easter" us. We will not die but live.

Comforter of those in need,
remind me that you are with me
during my times of struggle.
Be my hope as I wait to be raised
from the deadness of my difficulties.

Taste and See

■ **O taste and see that the Lord is good.** Psalm 34:8

What does it mean to "taste and see that God is good"? Many would think of the Eucharist. This is most surely a wondrous way of tasting God's goodness, but there are many other ways as well.

We can feed on our good memories and remember how we have been blessed with God's love through our relationships. We can be nourished by a moment of wonder and beauty and be fed by God's creation. We can experience the bounty of another's care and concern and taste the compassion of God.

The Easter season calls us to celebrate the Risen Life of Jesus. It is also an invitation to welcome life in a springtime world, to see the stirrings and marvels of death being overtaken by life. It is a time to taste the wonders of God's goodness in the seasonal cycle of life overturning death.

It is all too easy to be preoccupied with work and worries and forget to "taste and see." What will you "taste and see" today? How will you enjoy God's goodness?

Risen Christ,
my Easter world is filled with gifts,
both material and spiritual.
Slow me down today and guide me
to taste the wonders of your goodness.

The Extravagant Love of God

■ **See what great love the Father has lavished on us . . .**
        1 John 3:1 *(New American Bible)*

"*L*avished"—what a bountiful word. God's love has been generously shared with us, poured out abundantly into our hearts. We have only to be open and receptive in order for this extravagant outpouring of goodness to be ours. Have you ever thought about the profuse nature of God's great love? What a marvelous gift it is.

Some days it may be difficult to believe in this generous gift. It may not seem like we are lavished with God's love when we our experiencing our weaknesses or when life seems full of troubles and unwanted problems. Yet, this abundant gift of God's love never stops being offered to us.

John tells us that if we accept this lavish gift of God into our lives, it will begin to transform us. Like God, we will become generous with our kindness and acceptance of others. The goodness of God's love will shine through our lives.

Today close your eyes and picture God's love surrounding you and filling you with deep abiding peace and acceptance.

> *Bountiful God,*
> *what great love you daily lavish upon me.*
> *Thank you for your exceeding generosity.*
> *I will share this abundant love with others*
> *in my thoughts, words and actions.*

Meeting the Risen Christc

■ **When they had rowed about three or four miles, they saw Jesus walking on the sea and coming near the boat . . .**

John 6:19

We probably won't see something as phenomenal as Jesus walking across the sea today, but he will walk toward us nonetheless. Jesus will walk towards us in every person we meet as we go through this day. It is not on the Sea of Galilee, but on the "waters" of our ordinary lives that we will find him.

The disciples were afraid when they saw Jesus walk on the waters. Do we also have our fears about meeting Jesus in other people? Are we afraid that too much will be asked of our time and our attention? Do we feel inadequate or are we worried about what others will think? Are we concerned about our dislike or disdain of some who walk toward us?

The Easter season is an invitation to see with the eyes of faith, to see Jesus walking in our lives. To see Jesus is to see beauty where others might see ugliness in color of skin or ethnic background, to see hope where some would find only despair in illness and pain, to see goodness where another might see only the glare of anger and insult.

Jesus is walking towards us today. How will we welcome him?

Come to me on the waters of my life.
I will welcome you and embrace you
in whatever form you choose to be present.
I open my arms of love to you, Risen Christ.

Celebrating Easter Daily

■ **Very truly, I tell you, you will weep and mourn, but the world will rejoice; you will have pain, but your pain will turn into joy.** John 16:20

Remember the times you thought you couldn't endure the pain or the loss any longer? It seemed too much to bear. Maybe you are in a situation like that now. At such times it's difficult to believe that grief will be turned into joy. Others can assure us that the pain will pass with time, but usually everything in us doubts this. That's why we need to celebrate Easter continually. We need to recall and welcome the Easter story much more than just once a year. We celebrate Easter every time we look closely at the little surprises of joy in our lives. Each time we announce these joys to ourselves or to others, we are like the angels at the empty tomb announcing resurrection.

I know a woman who is never without the pain of four metal rods pressing in her back. Yet she has found joy beyond her daily pain. She relishes happiness in her relationship with her spouse, delights in her grandchildren, enjoys the beauty of the changing seasons. She is an Easter person who daily chooses to believe that she does not have to stay in the tomb of pain and discouragement.

> *Risen Christ,*
> *lead me to my own Easter moments.*
> *Clear my mind and open my heart*
> *so I can see the surprising little joys*
> *that are waiting to greet me today.*

Raised to New Life

■ **This Jesus God raised up . . .** Acts 2:32

*T*here is one lesson in particular which I learn over and over again. It is the truth that I cannot control the difficulties of my life all by myself. Usually my anxiety level has to reach an intense level before I admit to this reality. Each time I re-learn how necessary it is to throw myself into the arms of God, I promise myself that I won't forget again. But somehow I always do. I guess it's part of being human.

Easter is a wonderful reminder that we cannot get out of our troubles and our tombs all by ourselves. Even Jesus did not overcome his great obstacles alone. Jesus did not just rise up from the tomb by his own efforts. The Acts of the Apostles tells us that "This Jesus God raised up" to new life. It was the surrender of Jesus, heard so poignantly on the cross, that went with him into the tomb.

The Easter story assures us that we need God's guidance and strength and we need to let go of our own efforts to try to control life by ourselves. Let us place our hand in God's hand, and trust that God can raise us from our dead places just as Jesus was raised to new life.

> *Amazing One,*
> *there is much in me that needs*
> *to be raised from the dead.*
> *I place my trust in you*
> *to resurrect my lifelessness.*

Receiving Graciously

■ **God is able to provide you with every blessing in abundance, so that by always having enough of everything, you may share abundantly in every good work.** 2 Corinthians 9:8

I often feel that if I just had a little more solitude or a bit more quiet, I'd be able to do what I need to do for "every good work." I am always pining for larger chunks of solitude, more days on the calendar, longer hours in the day, thinking that would help my spiritual life unfold as I want. But the reality of God's grace being enough came home to me today in a letter from a friend. She closed by saying: "May God bless you with all the quiet you need, even if it isn't all the quiet you desire." "Yes," I thought. "God does give me all that I *need*, even if it isn't all that I *want*." If I would be fully present to God in my quiet times instead of thinking about how much more quiet I could use, I would be much more in tune with God and more satisfied.

Perhaps many of us feel as though we never have enough time to live our spiritual life adequately. Maybe we long for a deeper faith, for better relationships, for richer inspiration. Yet God is always bestowing upon us enough enthusiasm, generosity and truth "for every good work." Perhaps it is time to receive the gifts we have instead of focusing on the "not enough" pieces of our lives.

> *God of abundant grace,*
> *you are enough for me.*
> *I will savor the time I have*
> *and treasure my moments of quiet.*
> *Keep drawing me to your heart.*

Breakthroughs

■ . . . **blessed are your eyes, for they see, and your ears, for they hear.** Matthew 13:16

Jesus spoke about inner seeing and about the listening that leads to conversion of heart. He spoke about those who had closed eyes and ears. I can easily identify with this, for sometimes I really don't want to see or hear what needs attention in my spiritual life because it will take too much effort to do something about it. I usually do not consciously close my inner eyes and ears; rather, it's an unconscious or unaware process for me. What amazes me is how God manages to get my attention anyhow.

Not long ago, I was at church and heard an excellent homily on capital punishment. I found my complacency challenged as the homilist described Jesus as One who never used violence to fight violence. I had read about the issue of capital punishment, but ignored thinking about it from a Christian perspective. At that moment in church, my inner eyes and ears were opened. I hurried home and wrote letters to my legislators and then sent a donation to a group opposing the death penalty in my state. In one short talk, my inner eyes and ears were opened.

Compassionate One,
let me see with your eyes
and hear with your ears
so I can be a reflection
of your merciful love.

The Ascension: The Final Promise of Love

■ . . . as they were watching, he was lifted up, and a cloud took him out of their sight. Acts 1:9

*T*his scene is not unlike that of a family gathering around the bedside of a dying loved one to say a final farewell. If our loved one is the least bit alert, we wait for some final message or gesture that we can carry in our memory to last us a lifetime. In those last hours or days, we often struggle with mixed feelings—we want him or her to be free and at peace, yet we cling to the life and love we have known in our earthly relationship. At that moment, our hearts often carry a mixture of sorrow and hope.

The disciples must have had similar feelings as they stood there, saying farewell to Jesus. His message was a hopeful one, assuring them that they would not be abandoned. He promised that the power of the Spirit would be with them so they could carry on his work. It was a loving message—he believed they were capable and ready to continue what he had begun. So with us. The love we have known in the life of someone who dies can be carried on in our life. It is this love that makes our difficult farewells endurable and our grief consolable.

Compassionate One,
comfort those who are grieving.
Give them a sense of hope
like that given to the disciples.
Let them know that their loved one
can live on through their lives.

Be Grateful for God-Given Gifts

■ . . . why do you stare at us, as though by our own power or piety we had made him walk? Acts 3:12

After Peter and John had cured the crippled man, witnesses were astonished at how these ordinary people had done such a thing. But Peter is quick to point out that they did not do this by themselves. He told them that it was done by God's grace. This passage is a good reminder of the delicate balance needed between acknowledging and appreciating our own gifts and talents and remembering where they came from. This is very true in my life as a writer. I'm glad when readers affirm my work by telling me it is helpful for their spiritual growth. Yet I always want to assure them that it is not by my efforts alone that I write what I do. I could never write unless God had given me the gifts and was working through me.

Sometimes we deny our personal talents. It is false humility to do so because we are not acknowledging the generosity of God. At the other extreme, arrogance and pride are the source of convincing ourselves that we have done good things all by ourselves. When we speak the truth about what God has done to us and for us we need to do so with humility and gratitude.

Generous God,
thank you for all you have given to me.
Help me to use my gifts and talents well,
for your honor and glory
and the benefit of all humankind.

The Fire That Transforms Us

■ **I saw what appeared to be a sea of glass mixed with fire.**
                                            Revelation 15:2

*T*he Book of Revelation is not an easy scripture to read and understand because it is filled with symbolism. Because of this, the beauty of its message is often missed. In the symbolic vision of the victorious martyrs in heaven, two images tell of these holy beings: a sea of glass and a fire that penetrates it. Each image is a statement about the process of spiritual transformation that the martyrs experienced, and to which we also are called, in our own way.

A sea of glass is smooth, peaceful, almost transparent; it is like the peacefulness that eventually comes to all who have striven to be God-centered persons. This sea of glass is mingled with fire, symbolizing the transforming, purifying, and refining characteristics of divinity. Becoming peaceful and transparent is no easy thing. Living gospel values is a challenging and purifying process, for such virtues as patience, kindness, humility, and truthfulness do not come without a price. This is the fire that transforms us into peaceful, God-oriented human beings.

Fire of Transformation,
your grace continues to change me,
to bring me into the best of who I am,
until I am fully my true self and one with you.

Praying Constantly for Guidance

■ **Lord, you know everyone's heart. Show us which one of these two you have chosen . . .** Acts 1:24

*I*n reading my daily journal entries recently, I noticed how often I ask God for guidance and direction. I recognized how essential it is for me to turn continually to the Holy One so that I am both inspired and prepared to make good choices about how I live.

As I prayed today's passage from Acts, I thought, "It all sounds so easy—just draw lots and know which disciple is to take the place of Judas." On a closer look, I noted in verse 14 that this group "was constantly at prayer" and that they prayed before they drew lots.

It was their prayer that encouraged them to find someone to add to their number. It assured them that the Spirit would help them choose the person whose gifts were most needed. Their prayer opened their minds and hearts to accept the name that was drawn. We, too, need to ask for inspiration, guidance, openness, and acceptance in our daily prayer. We need discernment not just in special times, like the disciples in this case, but in each part of our day.

> *Spirit of God,*
> *open my mind and heart.*
> *Help me to make good choices and decisions.*
> *Strengthen my resolve to have prayer*
> *be at the root of all I am and all I do.*

The Gift of the Holy Spirit

■ **Did you receive the Holy Spirit when you became believers?**
Acts 19:2

*O*ne day I walked out of the house to go to a meeting. I had my hand on the car door, ready to open it. Suddenly a rush of peace and well-being swept through my spirit. I immediately had this keen awareness that someone was praying for me. I felt grateful and a bit in awe. I knew in that moment that God was filling me with love. This sense of an immense Power within us is one significant way in which the Holy Spirit acts. This powerful love stirs and calls to us. This gift of God's presence calls to us, unites us and supports us. We cannot force or control how or when this gift is given. We can only be open and ready to receive it.

We receive the gift of the Holy Spirit when we are baptized and continue to receive this gracious gift each time we are open to the goodness of God in our daily moments. It is easy to miss this graced movement of God or to take these moments for granted. Today might be a good day to deepen our awareness of how the Holy Spirit guides, protects, encourages, comforts, sustains, and draws us always toward a more complete union with our Creator.

Bearer of Gifts,
celebrate your presence within my life.
May your power be at the source of my actions,
in all my moments, no matter how ordinary.

Festivals

Draw Strength From Your Blessings

January 1 • Mary, Mother of God

■ **God, our God, has blessed us.** Psalm 67:6

*I*n the first liturgical reading for New Year's Day God tells Moses to share a beautiful blessing with the Israelites. Moses is to say to them: "The Lord bless you and keep you, make his face shine upon you, be gracious to you, give you peace" (Numbers 6:24-26). These are marvelous words that we could speak to our friends and loved ones, as well as to ourselves on this January first.

The Gospel also speaks of being blessed by God. Mary felt deep gratitude for her experience at Bethlehem. God blessed her with a healthy son. Visitors were in awe of her child. Angels glorified God at his birth. Mary treasured the blessings and pondered them in her heart. Mary's blessing would be her strength during the difficult events of the future.

As we enter a new year we, too, are called to ponder the blessings of our past year and to praise God for the treasures which are ours. These blessings can be our strength in the new year. Let us turn off the TV for a while, stop the noise of our life for a few minutes, and remember the ways in which God has brought us peace.

> *Mary, Mother of Jesus,*
> *teach us how to ponder our treasures,*
> *how to draw strength from our blessings,*
> *as we journey into this new year.*

God's Little Ones

February 17 • Seven Servite Founders

■ **The Lord keeps the little ones; I was brought low, and he saved me.** Psalm 116:6 *(New American Bible)*

*T*he Seven Servite Founders had much wealth and power. When they experienced a deep conversion of heart, they decided to give their riches away and move to caves on a hill outside Florence, Italy. There they prayed together and came to recognize their dependence on God. They walked through the streets of the city preaching about God and being attentive to the poor and the needy. These once powerful men became beggars, relying on others to give them what they needed. They were called "Servites," a word meaning "servants," and they dedicated their lives to the service of Mary who was also a "little one," as dependent upon God as were these beggars.

Becoming "little ones" took a tremendous amount of trust in God and a profound ability to let go of worries and concerns about the future. This is not easy to do. There is nothing wrong with having money and being free of financial concerns. We are all asked, however, to learn to be "little ones," accepting God as the center of our lives, being dependent upon divine providence, just as the Seven Servite Founders were.

Kind and loving God,
fill me with the courage and inspiration
to let go of my securities
when they keep me from following you.
May I become more trusting of your care for me.

Joseph, A Loving Companion
March 19 • Joseph, Husband of Mary

■ **When Joseph awoke from sleep, he did as the angel of the Lord commanded him . . .** Matthew 1:24

What must it have been like for Joseph to have walked the journey of life with Mary of Nazareth? He was a part of Mary's questions, anxieties, sorrows and struggles. He listened as Mary tried to explain the mystery of the Annunciation. He stood by her when she delivered the baby Jesus. He hurried with her to Egypt to save their child's life. He worried with her when their son was lost in the temple.

Joseph had great inner strength. He knew that God was his refuge and that he could count on God to be an ever-present help. We, too, have our "Joseph moments" when we are called to walk with someone who is anxious, or depressed, or seriously ill, or caught up in a life situation that seems overwhelming or intolerable. It is not easy to be like Joseph. We may greatly desire to free the other person from their struggles but be unable to do so. However, we can be patient, understanding, considerate and kind. We cannot do this by ourselves. We, too, need the inner strength that comes from drawing near to God.

> Joseph, husband of Mary,
> when I live with or accompany someone
> who is in great distress,
> I will try to be a loving companion
> as you were to Mary,
> always relying on God's strength to help me.

Consecrating Our Tasks

May 1 • St. Joseph the Worker

■ **Whatever your task, put yourselves into it, as done for the Lord . . .** Colossians 3:23

Joseph the Worker is usually pictured as a quiet, humble carpenter. What if he had been an extroverted plumber or a skilled dentist or an energetic administrator? It is not so much *what* Joseph did for his labor but *how* and *why* he worked. Theologian Martin Buber wrote that "it is not the nature of the task but its consecration that is the vital thing." Joseph, just man that he was, would bring to his work honesty, integrity and a sense of well-being.

Too often we judge ourselves or others by what we do rather than by the attitude with which we do our work. Work is more than making money, having prestige and finding success. It is an opportunity to use and share our God-given talents and to minister to the Christ who dwells in other people.

Do we put our heart into our work "as done for the Lord"? Is the quality of our work a worthy offering to our God? Let us unite with Joseph today and approach our work with gratitude for the talents we have been given. Let us consecrate our tasks to God.

> *Giver of Gifts,*
> *I consecrate to you this day all I am,*
> *all I have and all I do.*
> *I promise to use whatever talents I have*
> *for your honor and for the well-being of others.*

Learning to Lean on God
May 15 • Sts. Isidore and Maria de la Cabeza

■ **Ask and you will receive . . .** John 16:24

*T*oday is the feast of a farmer and his wife. I am a farmer's daughter and I shall always be grateful for my childhood days on the farm. Farming holds many joys but also many sorrows. Farmers know that they cannot control the outcome of their labors. They are daily pulled into the reality of uncontrollable weather. An insect infestation, an unexpected freeze, or a drought can destroy hopes for an abundant harvest. Yet year after year, farmers continue to plant and to trust that their work will produce something of value. Farming teaches the great need of dependence upon God. Those who work with the earth often count on the Divine Farmer to boost their spirits. Farmers know they must look to the Creator to help them accept what they cannot change and for support when they are discouraged and disappointed.

Many of you who read this will never have been on a farm, but you have uncontrollable aspects and issues in your life and work as well. You, too, have disappointing times. You, too, have to trust that if you ask you will eventually receive what you need.

All of us are dependent upon God.

> *I lean on you, Source of Strength,*
> *as I walk through life's ups and downs.*
> *I rest my burdens on the lap of your love,*
> *trusting that your compassion will uphold me.*

What It Means to Be a Christian
June 11 • St. Barnabas

■ **. . . it was in Antioch that the disciples were first called "Christians."** Acts 11:26

*S*everal years ago I spent a two-year sabbatical studying at a Buddhist Institute. It was the first time I had ever been in a non-Christian environment. At first, I felt both afraid and awkward, but I came to appreciate how others also long for a deep spiritual life. What most influenced me were the questions that arose out of my own soul—Who is Jesus? What does it mean to follow him? Do I have a strong relationship with this One who shows me the face of God? Such questions were very helpful to me and led me to a renewed appreciation of Jesus. I marveled again at the power of his compassion and the radical statements he made about loving justly and whole-heartedly. I realized that it was one thing to call myself "a Christian" and another to live as a Christian.

Barnabas, whose feast we celebrate today, was a "good man, full of the Holy Spirit and of faith." He lived when there was great enthusiasm for Jesus and his teachings. Now is a good time to dust off our own relationship with Jesus and to ask ourselves what it means to live the Christian path.

Spirit of Life, stir within me.
Set my heart more fully on Jesus
and inspire me to live this day
in a loving and just way.

Relying on God
June 24 • Birth of John the Baptist

■ **The child grew and became strong in spirit, and he was in the wilderness until the day he appeared publicly to Israel.**
Luke 1:80

*J*ohn had become a dynamic, no-nonsense person, a man of strong conviction. What happened to him during that time in the desert? It was a lonely place of solitude. It gave John the perspective he needed. John did not have other people to lean on in that sparsely populated place; he had to rely on God. John could hardly help but see how God was his true comfort and companion. He came to accept his gifts and to know that they were not of his own making. John learned of his greatness in the wilderness, and he also learned of his littleness.

Certainly John also had to confront his own "demons." There is no hiding out from one's self in the wilderness. The message he preached to others about reforming their lives he had first to learn in his own life.

We all need some solitude to be alone with ourselves and God. I grow concerned in this culture of constant noise and activity that we do not have the essential "desert" or solitude that we need to gain the necessary perspective on our lives. We, too, need the wilderness so we do not hide from God or ourselves.

God of the wilderness,
teach me who I am.
Lead me into solitude
and speak to my heart.

Spending Time With Jesus
July 22 • St. Mary Magdalene

■ **Mary Magdalene went and announced to the disciples, "I have seen the Lord"; and she told them that he had said these things to her.** John 20:18

*M*any stories about Mary Magdalene are not biblical, but they are told so often, people believe they are true. One woman told me she had read in the Bible that Mary Magdalene had red hair, but actually there is no account of this. These stories point to people's fascination with Mary Magdalene's character. What we do know of her is that she was a faithful, devoted disciple of Jesus, one of the few brave ones who stood at the foot of the cross at Calvary and who cared enough to risk going to her Teacher's tomb early in the morning to anoint his body.

What spurred Mary Magdalene to this tremendous dedication to Jesus, so much so that she would risk her life for him? I think it came from spending so much time with Jesus, listening to him speak to the people, observing his great compassion as he healed, sensing his deep bond with God as he went alone to pray on the mountainside. The life of Mary Magdalene calls to me in my discipleship, urging me to spend more time with Jesus as she did. My heart, too, can be ablaze with devotion and courage if I am willing to read the Scriptures and ponder the words of Jesus.

Mary of Magdala,
you were ablaze with love and devotion
for the Great Teacher.
I long to have my heart set on fire, too.

Be Happy for the Blessings of Others

August 6 • Transfiguration of the Lord

■ **Six days later, Jesus took with him Peter and James and his brother John and led them up a high mountain, by themselves. And he was transfigured before them . . .** Matthew 17:1-2

I never tire of hearing the story of the transfiguration of Jesus. It has such power and mystery in it. I wondered today about what might have happened "behind the scenes": how did the rest of the disciples feel about missing out on this profound moment of revelation? Surely they would have longed to have been on the mountain, too. I suspect that they had some feelings of envy, questioning why Jesus hadn't chosen to take them along. After all, they were also his disciples.

Sometimes other people have the things we long for: money, opportunity for travel, faithful friends, good health, a marriage partner, consolation in prayer, children who are successful, and so on. What happens inside of us when we see someone else receive something we wish we had? To be genuinely happy for another's "mountaintop experience" is a sign of a truly generous spirit. To enter into someone else's joy without wishing it was our own is a great gift that we can give another.

Friend of my soul,
help me to enter joyfully
into others' good fortune and success,
even when I'd rather have it for myself.

Sacredness of the Body
August 14 • Assumption Vigil

■ **Blessed is the womb that bore you and the breasts that nursed you!** Luke 11:27

*T*he Church recognizes the beauty of Mary's physical mothering and uses this verse to celebrate the vigil of her assumption into heaven. This feast proclaims that Mary was assumed into heaven with her body and soul, honoring her entire person as giving glory to God. It is an apt liturgical moment to reflect on the goodness, the sacredness of the body. Too often people have the notion that it is only our soul that is of value in spiritual growth. On the contrary, the body is a vital gift and a great help in drawing us nearer to the Holy One.

Mary's body was an essential part of her motherhood. Mary's womb carried the tiny seed of Jesus and brought him to birth. Her breasts fed Jesus the milk he needed as a newborn child. Mary's hands changed his diapers and rocked him in her arms. Mary's eyes watched Jesus as he learned to walk. Her ears listened to his first words. Mary's mouth kissed him and spoke comforting words to him. Like Mary, our bodies are an essential part of our life with God. Let us keep this in mind as we go through the day, noticing how what we see, hear, say, and touch can draw us closer to the Holy One.

Loving Creator,
my body is a wonderful gift.
May I appreciate my physical self
and care well for it.
As Mary's body brought you honor and glory,
so can mine.

Bringing Life to Others
August 15 • The Assumption of Our Lady

■ **In those days Mary set out and went with haste to a Judean town in the hill country, where she entered the house of Zechariah and greeted Elizabeth.** Luke 1:39-40

We know the story well. Young Mary, pregnant with Jesus, hastened over the Judean hills and valleys to be with Elizabeth, pregnant in her old age. Mary went quickly. She hurried to go to be with someone who needed her. Mary had a good excuse not to go on that journey: her own health and preparations for birth. But she risked the road. She took the time. She spent the energy. All of Mary's life was guided by the Spirit of God. Mary knew Elizabeth needed her, and so she went.

Mary's Assumption, a triumph over death, celebrates a woman who lived her life bringing goodness to others. Mary is a wonderful model of faith for us. In our world of hurry and worry, we can very legitimately have plenty to do just to care for ourselves and our families. But there are Elizabeths everywhere who need our visits. What a difference a phone call, a letter, or a "stopping by" can make to a lonely, ill or aged person. What joy we can bring to children by paying full attention to them. What happiness we offer friends and colleagues when we affirm their successes and celebrations. We need only to look and we will easily find an Elizabeth today.

Mary, delight of God's heart,
may the joy your visit brought to Elizabeth
be the joy that my presence brings
to those whom I take time to "visit" today.

The Faithful One
August 27 • St. Monica

■ **God is faithful; by him you were called into the fellowship of his Son, Jesus Christ our Lord.** 1 Corinthians 1:9

Monica, mother of Augustine, prayed unceasingly for the conversion of her son from his sinful ways. Monica knew she could not control, hurry or force God to intervene and override her son's free will. Augustine himself had to accept the gift of spiritual freedom which God was offering to him. Monica could only pray, trust and wait. Perhaps the greatest blessing of Monica's prayer was that it helped her never give up on her son. She always believed that he could grow and change. After many years of Monica's prayer, her son began to cooperate with God's grace and turned his life around. Monica's faithfulness with Augustine reflects the faithfulness of God who never gives up on us.

What was it like to long so much for her son to return to God? How did she cope with her heartache and sorrow? It was her faithful prayer to the God whom she knew would always be with her. This truth sustained her and kept her hopes alive. Many of us pray for others in the hope they will change. We cannot force them, but our faithful prayer can help us continue to believe in their ability to respond to God's grace in their lives.

St. Monica, your life teaches me
how to not give up on others.
Your life encourages me
to be persistent in prayer
and to always keep hope alive.

Learning From Our Weaknesses
August 28 • St. Augustine

■ **Where is the one who is wise? Where is the scribe? Where is the debater of this age? Has not God made foolish the wisdom of the world?** 1 Corinthians 1:20

Augustine's spiritual autobiography, *The Confessions*, is filled with depth and perception. His wisdom did not come easily, for sin and corruption filled his life for many years. When he finally let go and returned, he found God waiting for him. After this conversion, Augustine looked at what had happened in his life and wrote his "confessions" in which he described his return to God.

Augustine gained wisdom by reflecting on his experience and trusting in the mercy of God. We, too, have our own life story to ponder. Today is a good day to remember the many times and ways we have grown and learned from our mistakes, our blunders, our failures, our sins. What is our wisdom and how has it changed our lives? How have we experienced God's welcoming us home? Let us pray a prayer of St. Augustine's as we call upon God to transform us.

I call upon you, my God, my mercy,
who made me and did not forget me,
* although I forgot you.*
I call you into my soul,
which you prepare to accept you
by the longing that you breathe into it. (St. Augustine)

Doing Our Best Each Day

September 8 • Birth of Mary

■ **We know that all things work together for good for those who love God . . .** Romans 8:28

When Mary was born, her parents did not know the wonders for which this little girl was destined. All they saw was the miracle of life before them. They could never have envisioned the wonders which awaited her. Like all loving parents, they must have struggled to give this child a good home. As they did so, they probably had no idea how much their parenting of Mary would "work together for good," influencing her life in a profound way.

The same is true for us, whatever our position or age. We all live with mystery. None can predict how what is happening now will influence and affect the future. All we know is that we, too, are asked to trust that our loving efforts each day are of value in the eyes of God.

We are asked to have faith that our lives will bear fruit. It is not an easy thing to believe, especially if our lives are filled with pain or struggle or grief or a sense of meaninglessness. Look at the life of Mary today and remember how her parents also had to have courage and faith to live each day well.

Eternal Mystery,
I will live each day as well as possible.
Your grace will provide the help I need.
I leave the results of my efforts in your hands.

We Can't Hurry Growth
September 14 • Triumph of the Cross

■ . . . he humbled himself and became obedient to the point of death—even death on a cross. Therefore God also highly exalted him . . . Philippians 2:8-9

I sometimes tend to pass by the cross at Calvary and hurry on too quickly to the Resurrection. Knowing Jesus is raised from the dead and now triumphs over death, I can forget that Jesus felt no triumph as he hung on the cross. Rather, he cried out in agony, wondered if he had been abandoned and gasped in surrendering his last breath. In my own moments of trial and tribulation, I do not feel the triumph of the cross. I do not yet know the growth or conversion that awaits me. I need a belief that God will help me resurrect in due time, but neither ought I deny nor ignore the pain and darkness of the moment.

I think of this when I am with a family gathered by the bedside of a loved one who is very ill. They pat his or her hand, reassuring him or her that "all will be well." What a person also needs is someone to say, "What you are going through must be so tough." This compassion is a great balm for the one in pain. We must be *on* the cross before we can experience the triumph of the cross. We have the example of Jesus who gives us the courage to make our own journey toward resurrection.

Cross-bearing Companion,
journey with me when I am in pain.
Tend to my wounds when I am hurt.
I take courage from your journey
of death on the cross to wondrous new life.

Being With Others When They Hurt

September 15 • The Sorrowful Mother

■ **Meanwhile, standing near the cross of Jesus were his mother, and his mother's sister . . .** John 19:25

As Mary stood beneath the cross of her dying son, she must have been immensely grateful for those who stood near her. They could not take her pain away, but they would have given Mary great solace just by being there. Any of us who has been in a painful situation knows how consoling it is to have someone there who understands our hurt.

Influenced by my production-oriented Western culture, I have often underestimated the value of "just being there." Sometimes there's a voice in me that insists I have to *do* something. This voice questions the effectiveness of presence: Is it enough just to listen? Is it sufficient to sit by the bedside? Shouldn't I bring something? Can't I say something that will make a difference? Something deep inside keeps trying to convince me that if I just know the "right" thing to say or do, then both the hurting one and I will feel better. Sometimes words do help; many times "just being there" is most comforting and helpful.

Mary, Mother of Sorrows,
your presence at the cross of your Son
reminds me to be a good companion
to those who struggle on their cross of pain.
Assure me that my presence can be a gift
to those who are experiencing hurt.

Heeding God's Voice
October 4 • Francis of Assisi

■ We did not listen to the voice of the Lord our God in all the words of the prophets whom he sent to us ... Baruch 1:21

What would cause a young man from a wealthy family to give up all that he owned, including his own luxurious clothes? Falling in love could have that effect. It did on Francis of Assisi. He fell in love with God. He learned to listen to the voice of God through the insights and intuitions deep within himself. When God called, Francis responded by taking great risks. He chose to center his life on the One whom he loved, and he was willing to give up all his security to do it. Francis challenged the people of his time to live a simple life without greed. He encouraged them to love the earth and her creatures and to reverence God in one another.

As we celebrate the feast of this saint today, let us ask ourselves: have I heeded the voice of God in my life? Have I listened to God's prophet Francis? How much of this saint's challenge is a part of my life today? Are there ways I can live more simply, more deeply and more freely?

> God of love,
> in a nation of consumerism and greed,
> grant me the courage to ear your voice
> and to shed whatever keeps me
> from following you faithfully.

The God of Mercy and Tenderness

November 2 • All Souls

■ . . . **God will wipe away the tears from all faces.** Isaiah 25:8

*T*oday we remember our own deceased and all those who have died and crossed over to the other side of life. We come face-to-face with the mystery of what it is to die and enter the realm of eternal life. Do the deceased need our prayers? Do they continue to suffer? No one has ever come back to answer these questions for us. On this day we pray for a release of suffering for them—just in case they still have some pain on their journey Home. As we pray, the consoling and tender words of Isaiah assure us that God will wipe away all tears.

The Church wisely invites us to connect with our loved ones who have died, to remember them with compassion and prayerful care. This is the day to intentionally give our loved ones into the care of a God of mercy and tenderness. I pray in this way for the people in my life who are deceased: I remember what they looked like, and then I picture them in the arms of God. I see this Compassionate One carefully and lovingly wiping away any tears that might still be on their faces. I notice how God offers them a great welcome. I then entrust them into God's care and offer a prayer of thanks for the gift of having had these people as a part of my life.

> *Merciful and Compassionate One,*
> *I commend to you my loved ones who have died.*
> *May your mercy and your tenderness*
> *surround them and welcome them Home.*

The Poor and the Needy

December 12 • Our Lady of Guadalupe

■ He raises up the poor from the dust; he lifts the needy from the ash heap, to make them sit with princes and inherit a seat of honor. 1 Samuel 2:8

What a joy it was to celebrate the feast of Our Lady of Guadalupe at the Basilica in Mexico City. It is there that the cloak of Juan Diego, with its imprint of Mary, hangs for all to see. Pilgrims, many of them poor peasants, walk for miles to be able to view the cloak and pray beneath it. Their only wealth is their deep faith in God's abiding presence. Their joy is the bonding they feel with the Mother of God who revealed herself to one of their own.

I stood among these people on that feast and felt richly blessed by their presence. I felt God's goodness continuing to be revealed through them. I heard in my heart the words of Hannah's canticle: God lifts up the poor. I also felt a call to do my part to change the structures and systems that oppress the disenfranchised and impoverished people.

Mary, source of hope for God's lowly ones,
may I be bonded in love with those who are in need.
May I also do my part to work for justice
so that the poor will be lifted from the ashes of oppression.

When We Are in Darkness

December 14 • St. John of the Cross

■ **Are you the one who is to come, or are we to wait for another?** Luke 7:20

We are given the story of John the Baptist today to help us celebrate the feast of John of the Cross. Each experienced a time of doubt, yet remained faithful to God in spite of it. I picture Jesus' cousin, once so filled with zeal for the things of God, sitting in prison awaiting death, hearing about Jesus' teachings and miracles from the visits of his followers. Why, he must have wondered during his imprisonment, did the Miracle-worker not arrange for his rescue or release?

John of the Cross also had his time of questioning and doubting, a "dark night of the soul." He felt abandoned by God and fell into utter desolation. This "dark night" period was marked by purification of his soul. Eventually John discovered God as his Beloved and his relationship was greatly strengthened because of his bleak inner journey.

It is consoling to know that these faith-filled people had doubts and questions and that they went to Jesus with their darkness and confusion. Both prayed and continued to believe. It is good to remember this in our own times of confusion, doubts and questions about God's presence in our lives.

Faithful God,
you will never abandon me
in my times of utter darkness.
Let me see my doubts and questions
as opportunities to strengthen my faith
and expand my relationship with you.

The Joy of Being Close to God

December 27 • St. John the Evangelist

■ **We declare to you what was from the beginning, what we have heard, what we have seen with our eyes . . . 1 John 1:1**

John "saw and heard" Jesus, but that was not all. He had a deep place in the heart of Jesus. One of the few disciples who was with Jesus in such special moments as the Transfiguration and the Crucifixion, John was so close that Jesus entrusted him with the care of Mary, his mother.

There was a time in my life when I was afraid of being too close or too intimate with God. I was afraid that if I got too close, if I went too deep, God might ask something really difficult of me, like changing my life radically. Even though I prayed every day, I kept my distance. Then one day someone challenged me about this fear. I knew I had to change so I began giving up some of my walls and barriers. I slowly trusted God more. As I did so, I discovered, to my happy surprise, that the heart of God is big and deep and welcoming. Never has God asked too much of me. Always God has led me to become more of who I am meant to be.

Take time today to reflect on your relationship with God. Do you have any fears about being close to God? If so, talk them over with the Holy One who desires only good for you.

Beloved of my Soul,
I will draw close to you without fear.
You will never bring harm to me.
Draw me to your heart. I am ready.

Ordinary Time

Forgiving Another

■ **. . . first be reconciled to your brother or sister, and then come and offer your gift.** Matthew 5:24

*F*orgiveness is a very significant part of being reconciled, of being healed. Forgiving another is difficult. I like Jack Kornfield's definition in his book, *A Path With Heart*: "I will never put another human being out of my heart." I don't have to do this instantly, and I don't have to renew a relationship with that person—maybe the person in question has died or has abused me in some way. But I do need to come to a point where I do not wish that person harm. Until I have peace within myself regarding the relationship, I have not fully forgiven the other person.

Praying for someone I need to forgive or be reconciled with has helped me. I pray by simply naming that person, bringing him or her to God for a blessing each day. I don't specify what he or she needs. I let God take care of that. My intention is to make an act of love with a desire for each of us to find peace. I can't change someone else nor can I instantly get rid of all my unwanted emotions like anger or vengefulness. But prayer can soften the heart and open it. And that is what forgiveness requires.

> *God of Forgiveness,*
> *soften my heart,*
> *heal me of old hurts and wounds,*
> *and help me forgive.*
> *Bring me to peace.*

The Blessings of Daylight

■ **Fill us at daybreak with your kindness . . .**
Psalm 90:14 *(New American Bible)*

The ill or those unable to sleep at night are especially grateful at the first hints of morning light. The dawning rays bring freedom from the isolation of night's darkness and offer the promise of hope in the fresh new day. The author of the psalms understood the special spiritual moment of dawn and was in touch with the human condition. Many psalms refer to the morning as a time of blessing, an awakening to the graciousness of God, a restoration of hope, and an opportunity to realize again how blessed we are to have the gift of life. The spiritual writer Anthony Bloom once wrote: "This day is blessed by God, it is God's own and now let us go into it. You walk into this day as God's own messenger; whoever you meet, you meet in God's own way. You are there to be the presence of the Spirit . . ."

Whether we feel drowsy, grumpy, in pain, or energized and refreshed, ready to begin anew, when we awake with the dawning of a new day, we know that God is with us. The day that stretches before us is a day in which God will be our companion. It is a day in which we can bear the goodness of God to all we meet.

> *Bringer of the Dawn,*
> *I awake with gratitude for my life.*
> *May I bring the gift of your goodness*
> *to all those I meet today.*

Respecting Each One in Our Care

■ **Do not lord it over those in your charge, but be examples to the flock.** 1 Peter 5:3

"*L*ording it over others" means using knowledge or position to put others in their place. When people do this, it keeps them in control and gives them a safe distance between themselves and others. "Lording it over" comes out of insecurity, or over-responsibility, or arrogance, or fear. It is so easy to fall into the trap of acting like we know more, have more, understand more, or can do more than another person, especially if we feel threatened by him or her.

Peter is suggesting an attitude of reverence and respect for each person who is in our care. It includes a belief that everyone has something to learn and to receive from other people no matter what their age or situation in life. Parents can learn from their children. Pastors can receive valuable gifts of wisdom from members of their congregations. Physicians can discover new insights from their patients.

One of my life mentors in leadership was the late Bishop Maurice Dingman. He often said that when he went to diocesan and parish meetings he was there "to listen and to learn." What a Christlike attitude to have when we are working with others.

Great Teacher,
you can help me to respect each person.
I will open my mind and heart
so I learn from each one in my life.

Belonging to God

■ **We are from God. Whoever knows God listens to us . . .**
1 John 4:6

To belong to God means that we are "of God"; we do not exist apart from God. Thomas Merton described the false self as "the one who wants to exist outside the reach of God's will and God's love." The false self wants to be autonomous or separate from God, managing everything on its own.

When I can reap the benefits, I find it easy to belong to God. When everything is going my way and I have my life under control, I like belonging to God. But when I am in conflict with another person or want to focus all my attention on myself instead of sharing my gifts with others, then belonging to God becomes much more difficult. If I didn't belong to God, I could just follow my own will, living as if I didn't need to care for anyone else or pay attention to what God might want of me. Belonging to God requires that I accept not only the guidance, comfort, understanding and love God offers, but also the values and behaviors that go along with being one who is "of God."

> *I want to belong to you, God.*
> *to do your will, even when it means*
> *going against what would be much easier*
> *or more immediately satisfying for me.*

Invite Jesus Into Your Boat of Life

■ Then [Jesus] got into the boat with them and the wind ceased. And they were utterly astounded . . . Mark 6:51

Jesus walks on the water in the midst of a wild storm, and when he gets into the boat with his disciples, the storm yields to calm and stillness. Does this remind you of your own life? It certainly reminds me of mine, especially when I find myself pressed and overwhelmed with too much to do. Many a time I have reached the point of thinking I am going to be crunched by the "storm" of my busyness, and then I remember to pray. I mean *really pray*. I stop everything, close my eyes, and turn my total attention to the deep part of me where God dwells. I sit there awhile and unite with God. As I do this, I discover again that I can't manage my life without God's grace working in me. I remember who it is that has the true power and the vital energy.

It's quite amazing what happens when I deliberately invite God into the boat of my life. The wild winds of my inner self become calmer. My work goes better. I lose my panic and anxiety. I feel better about myself, and I recover my peace.

Thank you, Peace of my Heart,
for getting into the boat with me,
for calming the storms in my life,
for teaching me what a difference
your presence makes in my life.

Am I Ready to Meet God?

■ . . . he came to the Ancient One and was presented before him. To him was given dominion and glory and kingship…

Daniel 7:13-14

*H*ave you ever thought what it would be like to be presented to God? From time to time it is good to use our imagination to visualize what this might be like. We can learn a lot about our relationship with God and about how we are living our life. Author Robert Fulghum describes going out to his cemetery plot on every birthday to sit for awhile in a lawn chair and think about his presentation to God. From this challenging perspective he quickly sees what is vital and worthwhile in life and what is not.

We may not have to sit on a lawn chair on our cemetery plot to think about our "last days," but reflecting on this reality can be a good thing. Rather than being something morbid, it can help us anticipate union with the all-loving Being and review who and what is significant to us in this life. Visualizing our moment of being presented to the One who created us with love and who receives us with love can free us from some of the clutter and clutching of our lives and be a source of renewal.

Think about it: how do you envision your presentation to God?

> *Honor and praise to you, Ancient One,*
> *Ruler of my heart and my eternal Home.*
> *I look forward to the day of your final welcome*
> *when I am held forever in your loving embrace.*

Holy Wisdom:
A Special Guide

■ **For Wisdom is a kindly spirit . . .** Wisdom 1:6

*F*or most of my life I thought of "wisdom" as a quality of God. More recently, I learned how Wisdom is also a way of naming and addressing God. God not only *has* wisdom, God *is* wisdom. God is spoken of in this way in numerous books of the Bible, including Proverbs, The Wisdom of Solomon, Ecclesiasticus (Sirach), and other books called "wisdom literature." In these books, Wisdom is referred to as feminine, as "she."

I am drawn to a deeper appreciation of God when I read the descriptions given to Wisdom. Today's passage is no exception. Wisdom, a "kindly spirit," is one whose attitude and approach is always gracious, just, humane, and generous. The Wisdom of Solomon also speaks of Holy Wisdom as the "witness" of one's inmost self, and an "observer" of one's heart. Thus, Holy Wisdom is not only a caring, kind presence but also an intellectual guide and a discerning help for decision-making. Divine Wisdom will help us keep guard over our hearts and continually move us toward being truly loving persons.

> *Holy Wisdom, kindly Spirit,*
> *what a blessing you are.*
> *Thank you for constantly guiding me,*
> *for moving through my life*
> *in such a loving and gracious way.*

God Is Near to Those Who Suffer

■ **The Lord is near to the brokenhearted, and saves the crushed in spirit.** Psalm 34:18

So many things can break our hearts: people who set out to hurt or destroy us, natural disasters or other events that disrupt and change our lives forever, the deaths of dear ones, plane and car accidents, crimes that destroy our loved ones, illnesses that fill us with unending pain or leave us crippled, friends and relatives whose life choices or values greatly disappoint us.

It is not surprising that God is close to all those who are brokenhearted because God is, above all else, a God of compassion. This quality, more than any other, is the one that Jesus expressed in his life, in which he shows us the face of God. God is ready and willing to stand with those who suffer, vigilant with those who feel empty, discouraged or desolate. Even though we may *feel* abandoned by God in our brokenhearted times, God is very, very near to us, longing for our happiness and peace of mind.

> *Sheltering God, you draw near to me in my tough times.*
> *You reach out to me when I am most desolate and alone.*
> *You offer inner strength to endure brokenheartedness.*
> *Let me always trust in how near you are to me.*

Night Prayer

■ I . . . meditate on you in the watches of the night.
Psalm 63:6

*P*robably the only times one would pray during "the night-watches" are when experiencing insomnia, caring for a new-born baby, vigiling with an ill loved one or working the night shift. Most of us snooze through the night. But what about that time right before we get into bed? This can be a most fruitful time of placing ourselves in God's care, a wonderful moment of rekindling our bond with the One who ceaselessly watches over us. It is easy to neglect this significant time of prayer when our days are full of many wearying duties and demands, and our eyelids are droopy and ready for rest.

When I pray before bedtime, I begin by gathering God's angels around me: "Angels before me, guide and direct me. Angels behind me, guard me and protect me. Angels above me, keep watch over me. Angels beside me, care for and comfort me." Then I call upon the Spirit of God to be with me as I look over my day, to see how I have been aware of God's gifts. I generally have a lot of "thank yous" and usually a few "sorrys." I close by praying a few verses of a favorite psalm. This night prayer doesn't take very long, but it brings me great peace and joy as I hop into bed.

> *Guardian of the Night,*
> *I place myself in your care,*
> *knowing that your kind vigilance*
> *will be a comforting sentinel*
> *sheltering me within the darkness.*

A Strong, Positive Attitude

■ **Glorify the Lord with me; let us together extol his name.**
Psalm 34:4 *(New American Bible)*

*H*ave you ever noticed how another person's spirit or attitude influences your own? I was at a gathering recently and the person next to me was filled with negativity and criticism. She complained about everyone and everything. I found myself joining in with her. Her negativity fed mine. I left feeling badly about my behavior. I know it's healthy to voice legitimate complaints and concerns, but I also know it's lethal to the spiritual life when one gripes and criticizes incessantly. Life's wonderful gifts can easily be missed when life is constantly viewed negatively.

Then I thought of Sandra, a member of my Wednesday morning prayer group. When she comes into the room, she brings with her an aura of hope and optimism. She finds a lot to laugh about and looks at life in a positive way. It's not that she denies her own problems and troubles or that she never complains about life but she has a way of not letting herself get completely absorbed in them. I like being around her and feel uplifted and hopeful when she's there. Could this be why the psalmist today issues an invitation to praise and glorify God *together*? Could it be that the psalmist recognized how the strength of one positive, grateful person can draw another into similar gratitude and praise of God? I tend to think so.

> *Dear God, keep me from constant negativity.*
> *Fill my spirit with a resounding sense of gratitude.*
> *Help me to have a positive attitude about life*
> *and to find the joy hidden in little things.*

Staying Attentive to God's Word

■ **My mother and my brothers are those who hear the word of God and do it.** Luke 8:21

I am always amazed and grateful at how Scripture continually holds such stimulating and hopeful truths for spiritual growth. Jesus encouraged his followers to not only hear what he was speaking but also to take those words into their lives so that the teachings would transform them and their world. This passage reminds me that being "too busy" can get in the way of spiritual growth. When I am racing in my mind, I do not truly hear the word of God. I am not attentive in such a way that the transforming word reaches my mind and heart.

I often notice this when I am at Mass. Sometimes when the homilist refers to one of the passages, I realize that I missed hearing the Scripture reading entirely. My mind was off in "la la land." It's like being invited to a marvelous dinner table filled with delicious food—and not eating any of it.

It is not easy really to *hear* the word of God and it certainly is not easy to *act* on it, either. St. Ignatius of Loyola wisely encouraged those who wanted to hear the word of God to always begin by praying to the Spirit before reading and meditating on God's word.

Spirit of God,
help me be attentive to your teachings.
May I respond to them so they make a difference
in who I am and how I act each day.

Beyond Gloom and Doom

■ **When you hear of wars and insurrections, do not be terrified** . . . Luke 21:9

*L*ate one November I gave an evening conference on the theme of hope. Afterwards a young woman came up to me and, as soon as she began speaking, she started to cry. Between her choking sobs, she told me how much my words on hope meant to her. She said she had heard such "doom and gloom" from her colleagues and friends about the "end times," particularly in looking toward the millennium. She told me my words on hope gave her a much needed alternative viewpoint for courage and purpose in life.

For myself, I rarely reflect on the "end times" because I believe that whenever the "end" comes, it is vital that I be living my life as well as I can *right now*. I do think, however, it is good to be reminded that our earthly life will someday come to an end. When we pause to remember that we, too, are mortal and that death could happen at any time, it puts our life into quick perspective.

As a person of hope, Jesus would not want us to focus on gloom and doom. He was also a man of truth who would want us to keep our hearts in the right place, remembering that our earthly life is part of a continuum toward a fuller life.

> *Bringer of Hope,*
> *I turn to you with confidence*
> *that my life here on earth is of value.*
> *I will live close to your heart so that,*
> *whenever my earthly life comes to an end,*
> *I will be in harmony with you and at peace.*

In Giving We Receive

■ . . . the one who sows sparingly will also reap sparingly, and the one who sows bountifully will also reap bountifully.
2 Corinthians 9:6

What wisdom this verse of Scripture holds as Paul urges the Corinthian community to be generous with their love and service of one another. I had a good experience of this recently when the local hospice director called to ask me to visit a patient named Delores. Wouldn't you know, it was on a day when my office was a disaster and I was feeling extremely pressed by lack of time. Fortunately, God's grace led me to say "yes" instead of "no." I left my office reluctantly, however, worried about the deadlines of work that would not go away while I was gone.

When I returned home after my morning with Delores, I realized how much I had received in return for the few hours I'd given: deeper appreciation for my own health and the gift of life, a renewed compassion as I saw her husband struggle to be her key caregiver, and a sense of the strength and comfort that the love of her adult children gave her as they visited. That brief gift of my time helped me realize anew how rewarding giving can be when it is done with an open and willing spirit. And to my amazement, I had some renewed energy for my work and was able to meet my deadlines after all.

God of Love,
there are times when I need to take care of myself
and times when I need to serve others generously.
Help me to choose wisely how I use my time and energy
and to serve, always, with a gracious and loving heart.

Free Me From My Fear of Conflict

■ **Do you think that I have come to bring peace to the earth? No, I tell you, but rather division!** Luke 12:51

*J*esus warned that sometimes his teachings would bring conflict. This message is not appealing to me. I like peace and harmony. However, being true to the Gospel means I will have to stand up for what I believe, even if it causes division among those with whom I live and work. And it sometimes does as I try to take to heart what Jesus said about forgiving enemies, lending without expecting something in return, choosing not to be vengeful, not judging and condemning, and blessing those who curse us (Luke 6:27-42).

Should I be surprised, then, if what I say or do causes conflict? Should I wonder that not all will accept me when I speak out against such things as capital punishment, meager funding of programs for the poor, lengthy prison detainment of undocumented immigrants, and other issues that require compassion, understanding and loving kindness? Should I be amazed that my stance is sometimes met with cajoling, harsh words or silent dismissal?

Jesus, do not let my distaste for conflict
keep me from actively supporting and living
your profound and challenging teachings.
Help me to overcome my fear of disharmony.

Thanks for Each New Day

■ **Satisfy us in the morning with your steadfast love, so that we may rejoice and be glad all our days.** Psalm 90:14

*D*awn is the birth of a new day and an opportunity for entering into sacred communion with the Creator. As the darkness of night lifts and the rays of light open up the world to us again, we enter into a time that has a special quality of freshness and vibrancy. Each dawn is a miracle worth attending. Each morning is an opportunity to thank the Creator for our life. I am a "morning person" who enjoys getting up early, going for a prayerful walk, returning home and sitting in meditation. This time of day validates my hope and restores my gratitude for life. I have friends who are "night people" who stay up late and get up later in the morning than I do. Can they pray in the morning, too? Yes, they can. Morning prayer begins whenever we get up, not necessarily when the sun rises, but most certainly when we arise.

Each of us has to find the best time of day to pray, but I truly believe that one of the first things required for faithful union with God, no matter when or how we arise, is to pray some kind of thanksgiving for a new day. Life is simply too precious a gift to take for granted. It may be as simple as standing with hands outstretched with a loving heart, but a vital aspect of morning prayer is the intention to unite ourselves with the One who has given us life.

> *Creator of the Dawn,*
> *fill me at daybreak with gratitude,*
> *with a strong sense of your goodness*
> *and an amazement at the wonder of my life.*

What Do You Want?

■ **When Jesus turned and saw them following, he said to them, "What are you looking for?"** John 1:38

What would you say if Jesus stood before you and asked you the question, "What are you looking for?" Would you stand there in amazement, too awestruck even to respond? Or would all sorts of requests come floating forth from you? What would you ask for? Would you request miracles and answers to all your problems and concerns?

Anthony De Mello, S.J. tells a story in *Free Flight* about a woman who dreamed that Jesus was a salesman in a marketplace. When she asked him what he sold, Jesus told her that she could have anything her heart desired. She excitedly requested things like freedom from fear, peace of mind and heart, and the end of pain and struggle in her life. When Jesus heard this, he responded to her, "Oh, no, you've got me wrong. We don't sell fruits here, only seeds."

I've often thought of how much I want God to zap away every difficult thing from my life. Instead, God gives me "seeds" like wisdom, courage and faith so that I can grow and mature through my life's events.

> *Dear God,*
> *today I will pay attention to the "seeds"*
> *that are waiting to be watered and tended.*
> *I will stop looking for instant solutions to problems*
> *and be more aware of the opportunities for growth.*

Staying Faithful in Prayer

■ **My soul yearns for you in the night, my spirit within me earnestly seeks you.** Isaiah 26:9

*T*hree of us met recently for an evening of dialogue about our life with God. The two of us who were feeling much wilderness and emptiness in our prayer listened a bit enviously as the other person spoke about her insatiable hunger and longing for God. Everything in her life seemed to draw her toward the Divine. Her morning meditation was a period of deep satisfaction. Her heart was stirred constantly with ever greater desire for the Sacred Presence. She felt spiritually alive and alert throughout the day.

Later on, we two dry and empty ones described our journeys. As we did, we recognized that we were also yearning for God, except that it did not seem that way because we could not feel it. Yet our silent longing and hunger for God was keeping us faithful to our own spiritual journeys. We, too, were earnestly seeking God by our daily prayer and our continued openness to spiritual growth. When we are feeling dry and empty, we need to be faithful to daily prayer even though it doesn't feel very satisfying.

> *Faithful God,*
> *on my dry and empty days*
> *I will continue to unite my life with yours.*
> *I will be steadfast in turning to you*
> *no matter what my feelings might be.*

Love Yourself

■ **You shall love your neighbor as yourself.** Mark 12:31

This second commandment which Jesus proclaimed is a challenge not only to love others, but also to love myself well. After all, I am to treat others as I treat myself, and sometimes I treat myself rather shabbily. I do this when I do not allow myself enough sleep, fill my body with unhealthy food, overwork and get stressed, omit play and prayer in my day, forget to affirm and be grateful for my personal gifts . . . the list could go on and on. Jesus' commandment assumes that I love myself and that I am good to myself. On this basis, I am to be good to others.

I believe there are false messages in the back of our minds that keep us from living the second commandment. One message says that we aren't supposed to think kindly of ourselves because that would be pride. Another tells us that we should not give ourselves much attention or be too good to ourselves because that would be selfish. Yet if we are not kind and considerate of our own persons, how can we be this way with others?

> *Loving Creator,*
> *you have made me in your own image and likeness.*
> *My deepest being reflects your goodness.*
> *Nudge me to be kind to myself*
> *and to take good care of the gift that I am.*

The Two Ways

■ **Enter through the narrow gate; for the gate is wide and the road is easy that leads to destruction . . .** Matthew 7:13

*M*aking a choice for what is good often leads us along the road that is more difficult. We have most likely experienced this often in our lives. While the wide gate may look very appealing and inviting, our heart will always tell us what we need to choose. Often, that choice is for something we would rather not think about or want to do.

Jesus is not saying that positive, enjoyable and happy things will keep us from the Kingdom of God. Rather, he is teaching us that we need to make choices for good, and these are sometimes challenging and unappealing. It is not easy to love someone who seems very unlovable or to be honest when we could really use some extra money or to give up needed sleep to worship with the Church community.

What are the wide and narrow gates of your life? Look closely at them today. Which ones do you travel through the most?

Divine Gate-Keeper,
you guide me through the narrow gate.
Thank you for being my companion of courage
as I make choices to follow you with integrity.

Be Brave Enough to Trust God

■ **Lord, if you choose, you can make me clean.** Matthew 8:2

When Jesus came down the mountain, large crowds followed him. Among this huge throng of people was a leper who stepped out and asked Jesus to heal him. The power of Jesus was evident as he stretched out his hand and touched the leper. The "leprosy was cleansed immediately" (Matthew 8:3).

What was it like for the leper to make this request? Was it fearsome and overwhelming? Did he feel a tremendous vulnerability? Did he wonder whether Jesus would say "no" or push him aside? Was he mindful of the crowd's ability to beat or berate him? Many such thoughts and emotions must have accompanied the leper's decision to step forward.

Would I have been so brave? Could I have stepped out from the crowd to ask Jesus to share his power with me? Would I have had the leper's faith that Jesus could heal me? Do I worry too much about what the crowd might think? Can I overcome my doubts and fears and have faith that God will take care of me?

God's goodness and power are here for me. I must do my part and be receptive, trusting and open to receive.

> *Healing God,*
> *I step out from the crowd of my hesitations*
> *as I bring my hurts and woundedness to you.*
> *Stretch out the hand of your grace*
> *and bring me to greater wholeness.*

Speak From a Calm Heart

■ . . . **for it is out of the abundance of the heart that the mouth speaks.** Luke 6:45

*T*here have been times when I knew that what I was speaking to another person was a blessing of love and care. I knew this because my heart felt kindness and compassion. There have also been times when I knew that what I was speaking was causing great anguish and pain to another person. At these times, my heart was also full, but it was a fullness of anger, hurt or resentment. I have learned to look carefully into my heart during an emotionally charged situation before I speak in order to search out my motivations and my desires.

It also helps to pray that my heart has a strong foundation in genuine love. Jesus is always our model for this. He spoke from the fullness of his heart, and he spoke words of wisdom, care and compassion. He also spoke words of challenge and conversion, but these words were always spoken out of love.

Each night before going to sleep, it is good to reflect on the day to recall what we have said to others and to see what kind of fullness our heart has held. Only one question is needed: did my words and actions today come from a loving heart?

Heart of Love,
guide me when I am speaking and acting.
Keep me attentive and alert to my emotions
so that I will bring good and not harm to others.

Finding Fault With Others

■ . . . the scribes and the Pharisees began to be very hostile toward him and to cross-examine him about many things, lying in wait for him, to catch him in something he might say. Luke 11:53-54

I am always appalled at how verbally nasty human beings can be toward one another. That is, until I find myself doing the same thing! I always have very good reasons and excuses for why I want to catch someone else in their weaknesses. The hostility and plotting of the scribes and Pharisees isn't really all that different from my actions or from what happens in most human situations from time to time. The desire to catch others in what appears to be their weaknesses is very unkind and uncaring.

Two things help me to avoid this unloving attitude. One is to be more aware of the presence of God in the other person. I am not so quick to criticize and find fault when I really believe that God dwells within someone else. The other is to become more aware of my own motivations. Insecurity, hurt, revenge or the desire to feel better about myself can all be unloving motivations for naming someone else's weaknesses.

> *Gentle-hearted God,*
> *I do not want to plot hostilities*
> *and berate other human beings.*
> *May I live with your kindness.*
> *May I act with your gentleness.*

Abraham and Sarah's Faith

■ **For what does the scripture say? "Abraham believed God . . . " Romans 4:3**

God said to Abraham and Sarah: "Leave all that you've known, your security, your familiarity with the land and the people, and set out for something totally new. I can't tell you where exactly, or how you're going there, but trust me, it will be a good place. What's more, you'll have a child whose birth will bring forth many descendants for you." It's quite amazing, isn't it, that they actually believed God?

Scripture usually just gives us the bare bones of the story. We have to fill in the details. Can you imagine the talks (and arguments), the fears and anxieties that Abraham and Sarah must have had before they reached the decision to leave? Faith doesn't mean we never question or that we do not doubt or argue with God or that we push aside our human feelings. The important thing is that Abraham and Sarah went forth not knowing what exactly would happen with their lives. They only knew they couldn't predict and control the future and that they had to trust God's work. They finally just got up and went forth. They believed God. It was enough. It was what God asked of them.

> *What do you ask of me, Pilgrim God?*
> *In what way do you want me go grow?*
> *I will listen to you in the depths of my being*
> *and follow where you lead me,*
> *even when the path is unpredictable.*

Drawing Near

■ **Ah, soiled, defiled, oppressing city! It has listened to no voice; it has accepted no correction. It has not trusted in the Lord; it has not drawn near to its God.** Zephaniah 3:1-2

"The city" in the Hebrew Scriptures usually refers to Jerusalem. In this passage, the prophet Zephaniah is reproaching the people for not trusting or drawing near to God. This raises questions about our own relationship with God: How does one draw near to God? Isn't God always with us?

Yes, but it is much like a human relationship: we can live with someone, be with them all the time, yet not have much sense at all of what they are thinking or feeling. Maybe all we have are "take out the garbage" or "what time is dinner?" conversations. It is very easy to take our loved ones for granted and not spend much time in any in-depth sharing from day to day. To draw near to someone takes trust, believing they will want to respond to our efforts to share more deeply. It always takes a deliberate intention to try to connect with them on this level.

The same is true of our life with God. We must make a real effort to pray. We must be intent upon connecting with the One who dwells within us and "draw near" every day to spend some quality time with God in order to keep the relationship alive.

> *I draw near to you, Intimate One.*
> *You are the Center of my life.*
> *I desire to stay close to you,*
> *to communicate with you every day.*
> *I will try to not take our relationship for granted.*

A Little Light Goes a Long Way

■ **You are the light of the world . . . let your light shine before others.** Matthew 5:14,16

What a powerful affirmation—to be assured that we have this light within us that is meant to be shared. How many people believe that they are filled with the wondrous light of God? Like one tiny candle shining in a dark room, the light within can make a profound difference. When the light within one person is shared, it often brings what the heart needs most.

Recently, I received such a light through a visit of two widowers whom I had met only through letters. They were vacationing in the area and called to invite me to lunch. The light came to me through their openness, graciousness, hospitality and delightful sense of humor. I had been caught up in my own small world of busyness and studies. I didn't think that I could "fit" two more people into my life that day. Because I met them, however, I found a clearing space in my heart. I found communion in the simple and unpretentious humanness shining through the life of two caring strangers. They gave me joy and they expected nothing in return. The light they shared with me was truly the light of God.

Light of the World,
your radiance shines through us all.
May I be attentive, open and ready
to give and to receive your Light today.

All Christians
Need Patience

■ . . . lead a life worthy of the calling to which you have been called, with all humility and gentleness, with patience, bearing with one another in love . . . Ephesians 4:1-2

Why is it that being patient always sounds reasonable and relatively easy when I am feeling loved, rested and peaceful? It doesn't feel so easy when I am fatigued, discouraged, grouchy or at odds with someone. The last thing I want to do then is to extend extra forbearance and understanding to another. I especially notice my impatience when I am driving in heavy traffic. My hostile glares, beeping horn and muttered comments are enough to embarrass even myself! When I reflect on it, I see that my impatience usually happens when I am in a hurry, tired or thinking only of my own needs. That's when I most easily forget about "bearing with one another in love."

We always need patience. Each of us knows who or what challenges our ability to be graciously accepting and generous in our understanding. Sometimes we most need to be patient with ourselves. It is not easy to be patient, but it is a requirement of us who call ourselves Christian. I've found that I react and respond quite differently to others when I view them as they really are—a temple of God. Then I remember the dignity and respect they deserve. I remember to be patient.

Dear God, I need to be patient.
Slow me down when I am in a hurry.
Hold me back when I want to leap ahead.
Quiet me when I am much too anxious.

Returning to Jesus

■ Herod said, ". . . who is this about whom I hear such things?" And he tried to see him. Luke 9:9

*E*ven Herod—that "fox" as Jesus called him—was interested in Jesus and felt a keen desire to see him. What was—and is—so attractive about Jesus? Why do people feel so drawn to him? What has kept persons throughout the centuries seeking him and longing for companionship with him?

I have a great respect for the traditions and teachings of other religions, but I always return to Jesus and his message. Here I feel most at home, most inspired, most challenged to live my life well.

What attracts me to Jesus? His integrity: Jesus always lived what he taught. His compassionate presence: He extended love to all those who were hurting. His courage: Jesus risked his reputation and his life to speak out against the injustice and religious corruption of his time. His openness: He welcomed those who were very different from himself—lepers, Samaritans, sinners. All knew they had a welcome from Jesus. Love emanated from his being and his actions.

Ask yourself today what attracts you to Jesus. Spend some time with him, renewing and deepening your friendship with him.

Jesus, Friend and Companion,
thank you for walking with me
as I journey through this life.
I want to keep learning more about you
and to continue to grow in my love for you.

Living in the Present

■ **For everything there is a season, and a time for every matter under heaven.** Ecclesiastes 3:1

*T*ime is such an elusive thing and I find myself constantly wanting to control it. It seems like I am always "running out of time" when I am working at something which holds my interest. Sometimes my mind and feelings are far into the future while I am living in the present moment. At other times, I am clinging onto the present and not wanting to go forward. If it's a difficult situation, I want to hurry and get it over with. If it's a happy moment, I want to hug it to myself and not let it go. I think that I have a continuous tug-of-war with time.

The wise voice of the author of Ecclesiastes tells us that there is a time for everything. Each event and experience has some wisdom to give us if we are open and attentive to what it is offering to us. The present moment is what counts. Nothing else. Here is where our wisdom happens. Sometimes the only way we come to believe this is when we face a serious illness or the loss of something or someone significant. The quality of the present moment suddenly takes on a new look and becomes a precious commodity.

Eternal Love,
I desire to be less concerned about "having time"
and more concerned about how I live with the time
I have in the present moment. It is all the time I have.

Help From Our Friends

■ **Then some people came, bringing to him a paralyzed man, carried by four of them.** Mark 2:3

When I read this story, I thought of all those people in my life who have helped me grow. I may not have been flat down on a stretcher, but I was definitely in need of some help so I could get myself together and be more whole. I think of people who never gave up on me, even when I was complaining and constantly out of sorts. I think of parents, teachers and mentors who saw a potential for wisdom and leadership in me that I had no inkling was there. I think of my religious community members who offered me spiritual nourishment and the blessing of kinship when I was in need.

Each of us has been that person on the stretcher at some time. How blessed we are if there has been someone who cared enough about us not to give up on us. How thankful we can be if they somehow brought us to Jesus for greater healing and wholeness. Take a few extra minutes today to think about the persons in your life who carried you when you were on "the stretcher" of mental, emotional, spiritual or physical pain. Take time to thank God for these gifts, and if possible, write a note to one of these persons to thank them for helping you to be more whole.

Great Healer, thank you
for all who brought me to you
in my time of need and hurt.
May I do the same for others
when they are longing to be healed.

Patient and Persistent in Prayer

■ **Make me to know your ways, O Lord; teach me your paths.** Psalm 25:4

*R*ecently I asked a large gathering of retreatants to write down some of their questions regarding prayer. Quite a few wanted to know how they could tell if they were doing God's will. Others wanted to know if they were on "the right path." Psalm 25 suggests that we need to ask God for guidance if we are going to be living the ways of the Holy One. God can and will direct our paths if we are open, attentive and listening. For our part, we need to be patient, consistent in praying daily, willing to consult wise persons, and we need to regularly check our motivation—"Why am I doing what I do?"

St. Ignatius insists that a key way to know if we are doing God's will is to check on our peacefulness. We may not have many positive feelings about a decision or a direction, but if we have peace, we can be assured that we are probably in tune with God. We need to trust our truest self. No one else can tell us if we are on the path with God. Only our true self, that part of us that is in close union with God at the core of our being, knows this. Let us keep going there and trusting the Peace that resides deep within us.

> *I turn to you for light and guidance,*
> *Source of Truth and Peace.*
> *Teach me your will and make known to me*
> *how best to live with peace in my heart.*

Saving by Giving Away

■ **When she could hide him no longer she got a papyrus basket for him, and . . . she put the child in it and placed it among the reeds on the bank of the river.** Exodus 2:3

Moses was born when the king of Egypt had ordered that all the Hebrew baby boys be killed. In order to save him, the mother of Moses made the excruciating decision to give the little child away. As three-month-old Moses floated in the basket, he was found and given a good life with Pharaoh's daughter.

What must Moses' mother have thought as she placed him in that basket? Her heart must have been near to breaking. She could not have envisioned that her little son would be discovered by a rich woman and brought up among the elite. Nor could she have seen that this little endangered boy would be counted among the greatest spiritual leaders of all time.

Sometimes we must put our "little sons" in baskets on the waters of life and let them go into the care of God. Our "sons" may be whatever we love greatly and can no longer have: hope for good health, our jobs, secure situations, etc. When we give this little child of ours to the water, we cannot see what good will come of it. Yet the grace of God and the healing of time can bring us amazing surprises as it did with Moses. Next time we are asked to put our "little son" on the water, let us remember the story of Moses and trust in God.

Holy One, when there are things hidden
and unknown in my situation,
let me not doubt that good can come
from difficult decisions and courageous actions.

You Have Only to Keep Still

■ **Do not be afraid, stand firm . . . The Lord will fight for you, and you have only to keep still.** Exodus 14:13-14

*M*oses' advice to the Israelites came as they were fleeing Egypt with Pharaoh's army hot on their heels. Imagine how the people must have felt when Moses told them to "keep still," that God would fight for them. Surely, these were not easy words to accept as they ran for their lives and freedom. We know, of course, that God did fight and provided a way for them to escape their life of bondage.

"You have only to keep still." This is no easy thing when we are struggling to be in control and life keeps getting messier and more out of control. What happens if we stop grumbling and attacking our difficult circumstances? What happens when we are "still," when we turn to the One who promises to care for us? Our situation will not change instantly, but we will have greater peace of mind and more love in our hearts. Grumbling, complaining, worry and criticism never changed anything. On the other hand, trust in God, peace of mind and love in the heart have led to profound changes.

Dear God,
the next time I am "running for my life"
please remind me to stop and be still,
to let my heart and mind return
to the place of peace and calm within me.

The Seed in Rich Soil

■ **But as for that in the good soil, these are the ones who, when they hear the word, hold it fast in an honest and good heart, and bear fruit with patient endurance.** Luke 8:15

When traveling in the outback of Australia, I met an archaeologist who had recently been to the United States. He told me that he was in awe as he flew over the Midwest, seeing its rich soil and fields full of ripe grain. It was obvious that such abundance never came to the arid, sandy soil of the outback. No wonder Jesus used the image of "rich soil" when he spoke of the seed of God's word growing within us. He knew how easily and bountifully seeds would grow in that kind of soil.

God is always dropping seeds into our heart's soil. They are seeds of love, goodness, faithfulness, kindheartedness, generosity, integrity and many other Gospel virtues and values. These seeds will not take root and grow if the soil of our hearts is dry and rocky with attitudes of self-centeredness, indifference, envy, prejudice or arrogance. The seeds of God lie dormant in our hearts, ready to take root only if they are embraced. Today, let us peer into our hearts and check the soil to see if it is the kind that will allow God's love to grow.

> *O Divine Planter,*
> *I embrace the seeds of your love in my heart.*
> *I will nurture these seeds with my faith.*
> *I will water them often with my prayer.*

Fear of Rejection

■ **The stone that the builders rejected has become the cornerstone.** Mark 12:10

*L*ate one evening a pastor I know quite well called me. He is a kindhearted, generous man who cares deeply about the welfare of his parishioners. His voice that night was tense, sad, angry. He said he had just come home from a parish meeting in which a small but very loud group of people openly opposed his theology and his style of leadership. This group had hassled him for two years, and he had decided he had had enough. He told me he was resigning.

As I listened to him, I thought of my own tendency to want to run away from those who reject me or my message, especially when these people are not open to change. It is ironic, though, that we who profess to follow in Jesus' footsteps never want to do so when it means experiencing the rejection which Jesus experienced. The one who follows Jesus and speaks his message can expect some rejection because the message of the Gospel is not an easy one to hear or to accept. The true disciple ought not give up easily.

> *God of Courage and Wisdom,*
> *be my strength when I want to give up*
> *in the face of rejection or challenge.*
> *Guide me to know when to "hang in there"*
> *and when to say "enough" and move on.*

Unpleasant Thoughts

■ **On one occasion when Jesus was going to the house of a leader of the Pharisees to eat a meal on the sabbath, they were watching him closely.** Luke 14:1

Whenever I read of Jesus being constantly scrutinized, criticized and pressured by harsh judgments, I think of how I would never have done that had I known him. Then something happens to remind me that I am not all that different from the Pharisees.

Recently, I was in a grocery store and I saw a woman who looked like someone I had known who had treated me harshly. I began thinking about this woman and soon all kinds of negative thoughts flooded my mind. This continued until I drove home, got out of the car—and realized that I was so busy thinking unpleasant thoughts about that woman that I had completely forgotten to bring home my bags of groceries!

I laughed right out loud when I saw what I had done, and I said, "Okay, God, you got me." I instantly recognized how self-absorbed I had been in something similar to the Pharisees, judging unlovingly and looking at another's life with an unkind viewpoint. It taught me a good lesson to be more careful about the negative energy that can easily creep into my thoughts and feelings.

Spirit of love,
how easily my judgmental thoughts
can lead me astray from your love.
When I focus on others' failings,
return me to positive thinking.

Releasing Unwanted Emotions

■ **And he sighed deeply in his spirit and said, "Why does this generation ask for a sign?"** Mark 8:12

*I*n giving retreats, I see again and again how people struggle with their unwanted emotions such as anger, impatience, discouragement, irritation, envy. I draw comfort from knowing that Jesus had some of these feelings. The Pharisees were arguing with him, seeking a sign to test him, when this sigh came from deep within him. This was a genuine human emotion of Jesus. And it happens to all of us at times.

One of the keys to unwanted emotions is to not let them have power over us, not allow them to take up all our time and energy. Sighing is a good way to breathe out inner turmoils. Scientists note that sighing is a healthy stress reliever. There are also other ways to release unwanted emotions. We can talk to someone about them or write about them. I find it helpful to return to the psalms. Many of our unwanted emotions are voiced in the psalms, and that helps us to see that we are not alone in how we feel. No matter how awful the psalmist's feelings, the psalm ends on a note of hope, a firm trust that God will shelter and protect the one who is hurting and upset.

> *When I am engulfed in misery,*
> *sigh deeply within me, Healing Spirit.*
> *Restore a sense of emotional balance*
> *in the realm of my deepest self.*

A Prayer for Self-Esteem

■ **You do well if you really fulfill the royal law according to the scripture, "You shall love your neighbor as yourself."**
James 2:8

The royal law of loving others as ourselves is quite a challenge. First of all, it requires us to love ourselves well. I meet many, many adults who struggle with their self-worth. If they make mistakes, they call themselves "stupid." If they don't match up to what people think is the right physical size, shape or color, they consider themselves "ugly." If they say the wrong thing or lack some social skill, they abuse themselves verbally and feel guilty or ashamed.

St. Teresa of Avila developed a prayer that I find very helpful in gaining self-esteem. Sit in a chair and imagine Jesus looking upon you with great love. That's it. Just sit there and be loved. This is not easy at first, but gradually, day after day, it becomes less difficult and more acceptable. As we learn to love ourselves more, we will find that it is much easier to love others in a non-judgmental way as well.

> *Gracious One,*
> *you look upon me with great acceptance.*
> *On those days when my personality flaws*
> *glare at me and shake their fists,*
> *help me to extend kindness toward myself*
> *and to receive your unconditional love.*

Ride Out Life's Storms

■ **Lord, save us! We are perishing!** Matthew 8:25

We all have "violent storms" in our lives at one time or another. They take the form of illness, death of loved ones, unexpected painful events, broken relationships, struggles within us or with those we love. Sometimes these violent storms last only a day, but sometimes they are excruciatingly long. What do we do when violent storms come? How do we respond on a spiritual level?

When the disciples got caught in the storm, they did not trust that the presence of Jesus would be enough for them. They panicked, and Jesus chided them for their lack of faith: didn't they believe that if he was with them they would be safe? Did they not know by now that he would be there for them in the scary moments of their lives?

Similarly, one of our first instinctive responses to our own storms is a fear-filled desire to be rid of the storm as quickly as possible. We may plead with God to get us instantly out of the pain or mess we are in. It might be better simply to place our hand in the hand of our Divine Companion and say, "I trust that you will be with me through it all. I trust that you will be my strength and support. I believe that you will care for me and ride out the storm with me."

I place my hand in yours, O God,
and I let peace flow into my mind and heart.
You have promised that you will be with me
in the storms and in the calm times, too.
Let me not doubt the power of your love.

Index of Scripture Passages

Index of Scripture Passages (continued)

Also by Joyce Rupp . . .